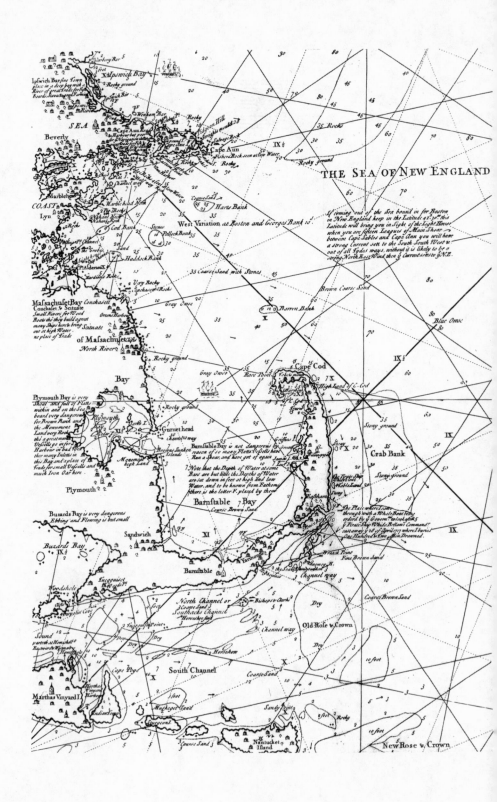

The
PIRATE PRINCE

Discovering
the Priceless Treasures of
the Sunken Ship *Whydah*

AN ADVENTURE

Barry Clifford

WITH

Peter Turchi

PRODUCED BY THE PHILIP LIEF GROUP, INC.

SIMON & SCHUSTER
New York   London   Toronto   Sydney   Tokyo   Singapore

SIMON & SCHUSTER
Simon & Schuster Building
Rockefeller Center
1230 Avenue of the Americas
New York, New York 10020

Designed by Irving Perkins Associates
Manufactured in the United States of America

1 3 5 7 9 10 8 6 4 2

Library of Congress Cataloging-in-Publication Data
Clifford, Barry.
The pirate prince: discovering the priceless treasures of the sunken ship *Whydah* / Barry
Clifford with Peter Turchi.
p.   cm.
Includes appendix and index.
1. Whydah (Ship)   2. Shipwrecks—Massachusetts—Cape Cod.   I.Turchi, Peter, date.
II. Title.
G530.W5787C57   1993   93-16266
974.4'92—dc20   CIP

ISBN 0-671-76824-7

Published by arrangement with The Philip Lief Group, Inc.
6 West 20th Street
New York, New York 10011

PAGE 2

Captain Cyprian Southack's rendering of the wreck site. A meticulous catographer, Southack's measurements proved vital in providing clues to the location of the *Whydah* more than three hundred years later. *Houghton Library, Harvard University*

To my brave and loyal brethren
who ventured out with me
to where the Earth dropped off
and found the greatest treasure of all:
true friendship

To them,
and especially to Ken Kinkor, Bob Lazier,
Todd Murphy, Allan Tufankjian,
and my family,
the following narrative is dedicated.

B.C.

My work on this book benefited greatly from the generous cooperation of not only Barry Clifford but also John Beyer, Stretch Gray, Chris Hamilton, Todd Murphy, and Ken Kinkor, and from the research and writing of Jacqueline Coleman; it would not have been possible without the support and encouragement of Laura, my wife.

P.T.

CONTENTS

The
PIRATE PRINCE

PROLOGUE: PANAMA

Care killed a cat. Fetch ahead for the dubloons.

—Long John Silver, *Treasure Island*

To say PEDRO VALENCIA WAS wet is to say a rock is hard.

He had made the mistake, just a few minutes earlier, of lifting his hat; he meant only to wring out the hair trailing over his forehead in order to keep the trickling water from his eyes, where it obscured his vision of the rain. In that short time the one part of his body that had been dry, the top of his head, was drenched. Rain pattered through the trees, dripping from leaves and vines; on the ground, water rushed from the mountains, carving streams, leaping gullies, seeking out the river far below. His coat weighted him down, his cotton shirt stuck to his chest, and his toes nestled in fungus.

But the water was nothing compared to the mud.

The jungle offered obstacles enough to a man; to a mule train it was impassable. Pedro had no choice but to lead his animals along the Camino Real, the Royal Road, in which the mud—which was not even solid mud but a thick ooze that yielded with every step, and flowed yellow with the urine of the mules—was interrupted only by moss-covered rocks, each of which tempted man and beast with the promise of sure footing but which was, Pedro knew, even more dangerous. Under the torrent of rain, the sloping hillside to the left of the camino threatened to collapse and cover the path at any moment. As it was, the mules often stopped and patiently waited while Pedro and his men moved mud-covered trees from the road.

At night the men cleaned their mud-spattered guns in preparation for the puma that preyed on the mud-covered beasts.

Glancing down at the river, Pedro felt the slime squeezing through his boots and, when he once again pushed aside the wet hair above his eyes, the water running down his cheeks. Coming to a turn in the path, he saw that a section of the road he had walked on last month no longer existed.

This was not unusual.

"Slowly," he called out.

Turning to the animals behind him, he noticed a tarantula the size of his hand at the edge of the road.

"Do not bother us," he told it. "We have trouble enough without you." Personally, he had nothing against the spiders; one of his men, Ramon the crazed storyteller, had even carried one as a pet. Pedro reserved his contempt for the snakes, so lazy they only crawled. He carried a stout walking stick in part for balance, but also to engage vipers and their cousins. After letting a snake coil itself around the stick, he would fling it high into the air over the river, shouting, "If you won't walk like a man, fly like a bird! Swim like a fish!"

A wild snort interrupted his meditation.

Even as Pedro turned, he knew what had happened. One of the mules had misstepped, falling off the path.

"Stop!" Pedro called back. "Calm the others."

In fact, the rest of the mules seemed unconcerned with the fate of their colleague. They stood silent in the ceaseless rain.

Roberto and Luis joined Pedro at the edge of the road.

"*Mala suerte,*" Luis said. "Bad luck."

"*Muy mal,*" Roberto agreed.

The cliff where they stood plunged perhaps one hundred and twenty feet to the Rio Chagres, in this season a wild river, muddy and deep.

Unfortunately, the mule had only fallen a third of the way.

Luis said, "No man could safely descend the slope."

Roberto added, "Even if he could, it would be unreasonable to ask him to carry back a fully loaded animal."

The three men watched the mule struggle, kicking into the mud, seemingly unaware that the thrust that enabled it to stand would also send it plunging to its death. The load on its back and its own struggle forced the animal slowly downward.

"Bring me a rope," Pedro told Luis.

The young man obeyed silently. When he returned, however, he spoke solemnly. "I am younger and stronger. Also, due perhaps to a lack of ambition, I cannot begin to compare my meager belly to the generosity of your own. Therefore, I will climb down, leaving you and Roberto, my strong and trusted friends, to pull me back."

Roberto said, "I will pull as if my own mother's life depended on it."

Pedro weighed the rope in his hands. At the first step on the cliff, a man would be forced to his hands and knees; they would no more be able to pull a fighting mule up to the road than drag a dark cloud down from the sky.

"This animal's burden is my responsibility," he told Luis. "As are you. I must go."

Pedro tied the rope around his waist, feeling it slip through his fingers, anticipating its slide through the hands of the two younger men. Several things could happen: stepping off the cliff, he could immediately drop to his death. If Roberto and Luis did not entirely lose their grip, he might tumble past the mule, reaching the river alive, only to drown; he could not swim. Or he could successfully reach the mule and, in unstrapping its load, be kicked to death.

"We pray for your safety," Luis said.

"*Gracias,*" Pedro told him. "But, *por favor,* I would ask you to do nothing to distract your concentration from the rope."

But Pedro Valencia's loyalty to his employer was tested no further that day. As he took his first step from the road, the animal below reared up, wavered momentarily, dropped to the river, and sank.

"Water snakes." Stretch ducks beneath a branch as he follows the guide half his height. "That's all anybody told me about."

"He said vipers," Murphy insists. "That day we met at the house with all the books, he specifically mentioned vipers."

We are somewhere in the mountains of Panama. I have a map, but here in the jungle that's as useful as a sundial in a cave, so I'm counting on our new guide. The first guide wanted nothing to do with treasure lying at the bottom of dark, cold river pools; he wanted to introduce me to friends of his, grave robbers.

But I choose my own adventures. Panama is wild territory; Manuel Noriega's homeland. The guide we're following now carries a knife that hangs halfway to his knee.

"I don't mind snakes in the water," Stretch says. "As long as I'm in a wet suit, and they're no bigger than I am, I can deal with that. But I don't want to be asleep one night and feel this long thing sliding—"

"You're such a wimp," Murphy tells him.

Something rustles off to my right. "What was that?"

Our guide shrugs. "Monkey, ocelot, *tigre.*"

We continue walking.

"And leeches," Stretch says. "I know, doctors used to use them to bleed their patients. But most of those people died, right?"

At the close of the fifteenth century, after Columbus expanded the limits of the known world, Spain and Portugal went to Pope Alexander to resolve their differences. The pope assigned to the heirs of Ferdinand and Isabella most of the new-found regions west of the Atlantic, and Spain soon discovered that her new territories contained seemingly infinite riches. In the next 150 years or so, the Crown received shipments of gold and silver ore worth approximately $18 billion. When you handle that sort of money, some of it's bound to drop through the cracks.

That's where I come in. For the past ten years I've been a professional treasure hunter. Treasure can be more than gold coins spilling out of a chest; I've traveled around the world looking for everything from Revolutionary War ships to missing airplanes to copper cable lying on the floor of the ocean. Before I start looking, though, I do a lot of detective work—reading between the lines of books, researching old records, and talking to people whose stories might reveal that one crucial detail, something even they may not realize is the key to the mystery.

The metals mined in Mexico were carried by mule train from

Mexico to Veracruz to meet the fleets carrying it to Seville; metals from Peru went to Panama, on the Pacific Coast of the isthmus, then made the treacherous thirty-mile land journey to the port city of Nombre de Dios. All the treasure found off the Florida Keys in the 1970's and 1980's, including the *Atocha,* was just a tiny part of the treasure carried on Spanish ships. The mines of Peru alone, during King Philip II's reign, annually produced $12 million worth of gold. Every year two treasure convoys arrived in Spain, one from Havana, the other from Nombre de Dios—some seventy ships. Some were attacked by pirates; still others sank in storms farther out to sea. But plenty of Spanish gold never even made it that far.

That's why we're in this hot, muddy hell—to pick up where someone else left off.

In 1572, Francis Drake set out to destroy Spain and line his own pockets—not necessarily in that order—by attacking Nombre de Dios. (This was eight years before he became, thanks to a few wrong turns, the first Englishman to circumnavigate the globe.) After sailing the Atlantic, Drake and his men took the town in the predawn hours of a late-July morning. As the local people began to awaken, Drake led a small group of men to the governor's house where, on the ground floor, they saw an amazing, once-in-a-lifetime, dream-come-true sight: silver bars stacked solid in a block seven feet by ten feet by twelve feet high—360 *tons* of silver—

—and cursed their luck.

Why?

Because that wasn't the treasure.

Drake knew the silver was nothing compared to the gold—and the gold wasn't in the governor's house, it was in the king's Treasure House.

There's a lesson to be learned from the rest of the story, but you can decide for yourself whether the lesson is about fate or greed or loyalty or the worth of a good map.

A storm broke out. The Englishmen ran for shelter under a penthouse at one end of an impressive building. While they waited for the lightning and rain to stop, drying their muskets, they snooped around and saw—but you're ahead of me here—the building they were huddled beside was the Treasure House. Just as Drake gave orders to begin moving the gold, the townspeople launched a counterattack.

Drake was wounded; his boot filled with blood, he left crimson footprints on the sand. Before he left many, though, he passed out. By the time he revived, the battle had turned against the English, but his crew refused to abandon him. Against his protests, they carried their captain back to the ship, sacrificing the treasure.

Years later, as a relatively old man, Drake returned to Nombre de Dios with two thousand men in six ships. In the meantime, though, fever had struck; the town was all but abandoned. While Drake and some of the men set about digging up jewelery and plate hidden in the forest by the fleeing townspeople, one of his officers, Thomas Baskerville, led a group to attack Panama City, at the head of the overland trail.

Nothing doing.

The weather was terrible; the men slogged through mud, saw their rations spoiled by rain, found the treacherous path blocked by trees dropped by the Spanish, were pinned to the ground by snipers and, while deciding whether to attempt the impossible, discovered their matches and gunpowder were soaked, useless.

Understand, Baskerville was no quitter. He and Drake made new plans to take Panama, and no doubt would have tried again—but the diseases in Nombre de Dios spread to the ships, killing a great many of the men, including Drake himself. Baskerville led the survivors home, empty-handed yet again.

So Stretch and Todd Murphy and I are searching for the treasure lost by mule drivers on the Camino Real over the course of 150 years. The Spaniards, obviously, didn't dive, and the local Indians refused, saying the pools were too deep and cold. It wasn't their money.

Each mule carried approximately two hundred pounds of silver. Silver is selling for roughly $40 an ounce as I write this, which would make each mule-load worth $128,000. When you consider that finding it is only a matter of sending divers into the mountain pools in dry suits with hand-held metal detectors, the return on the investment isn't bad.

But it's not just about money. I want to find a part of what was the most magnificent treasure on earth, the source of Spain's greatness. I want to hold what Drake saw but didn't have the chance to touch.

One of the things I like about treasure hunting is that if you work hard enough and have enough patience, or stubbornness, you can beat the odds. And there's more treasure lying around than you might think. My first great discovery, the pirate ship *Whydah*, lay off the coast of Cape Cod in Massachusetts—not all that far from where I spent my summers as a boy, listening to pirate stories and staring out at the ocean, imagining finding treasure one day.

THE LEGEND

My UNCLE BILL WAS THE best storyteller in the world.

Bill Carr, my mother's brother, was the one who first told me about Black Sam Bellamy. Uncle Bill started telling me about Bellamy, the pirates who sailed under him, the *Whydah,* and Maria Hallett, the young woman who haunted the cliffs of the cape awaiting his return, when I was less than five. Since then I've heard dozens, hundreds of variations.

For example, some people claim Maria Hallett never existed. Others say court records tell us when she was born, when she died, and how her estate was settled. The Maria Hallett whose records I've found died with a gold necklace in her possession—an unusual piece of jewelry for an outcast seamstress to own. The people who believe the legend point out that there is today—you can see it for yourself—a restaurant called Goody Hallett's just north of Wellfleet—but the critics add that it isn't far from a restaurant called Moby Dick's.

Among the people who allow that Maria existed, some say she had beautiful yellowish-blond hair, others say it was as black as Bellamy's. Some say she committed suicide over the death of her lover; others say she actually caused the wreck by cursing his ship; still others say she lived on to doom sea captains for years, and continues doing so today. Who knows whether it was really love that made Bellamy hug the cape that night? One of my good friends, a specialist in pirate history, is absolutely convinced Maria existed, only he says her name wasn't Maria.

Every old-timer on the cape has his or her own idea about what really happened, or what should have happened. Uncle Bill heard his stories from people older than he was, now dead and gone, and they had heard them from their parents and uncles. Bill spent a lot of his time in an old fishing shack covered with vines and, where you could still see them, weather-beaten cedar shingles worn gray. Inside, rotted fishing nets lay piled on the floor. The old rope seemed to radiate heat, so my cousins and I lay on them, keeping warm, smelling generations of fish, and listened to Bill's story.

Drinking a cup of tea by the rail of the most magnificent ship he had ever sailed, with nearly five tons of treasure under his feet and a gold ring holding a perfect emerald in his pocket, Sam Bellamy—known as Black Bellamy, for his wild mane—saw his dream coming true. If life hadn't turned out exactly the way he had planned, in some ways this was even better.

Since just before dawn, over four hours now, they had been in pursuit of a cargo ship. Moments ago Bellamy had ordered the captain to strike his colors and surrender. He obeyed. The *Mary Anne* was his.

Now he told Burke, his bos'n, "Send Baker to command, and Brown. Give them four or five others."

"Aye, Captain."

Bellamy worried a loose tooth with the tip of his tongue. Despite the bank of clouds building on the horizon, he would stay close enough to go ashore tomorrow. What concerned him—this man who didn't hesitate to command scores of others, this captain who had quickly built a reputation for bravery and daring—wasn't the ship they had overtaken or the approaching storm, but—and he had told no one about this, *no one*—a woman.

Two years earlier, as an impoverished young sailor, he had gone to Cape Cod to search out relatives. One day he had walked from his lodging in Higgins' Tavern, by the Burying Acre, to 'Tarnity Briars where, beneath an apple tree so full with blossoms it looked like a white cloud descending, a young girl sang with the voice of an angel. He introduced himself; she responded, not shyly but eagerly: her name was Maria Hallett. By nightfall they were lovers.

Over the next days and weeks he told Maria his plan to sail south, past the coast of Florida, to raise the treasure from the Spanish Fleet that had sunk in the Carribean laden with over two thousand chests of newly minted silver coins.

"There's something else," he told her. "I mean to captain a ship of free men—men who choose to sail, who have a voice in establishing the conditions under which they work." Of course, he'd need a patron, and a crew, and a vessel.

Maria believed in him.

She had heard all the fishermen and dreamers on the cape talk about sailing for treasure, but she believed he was the one who could do it. Before he set off, he made her a promise.

"I'll return for you," he said as they sat looking over the ocean. "I'll come sailing the longest, tallest ship you've ever seen—but not the fastest."

"No?"

"She'll be so laden with gold and silver she'll need wind in every sail to reach you. The hold will be so full, chests of coins will spill out onto the deck. But in here"—he rolled to his left, opening the buckle on his three-cornered pocket—"I'll have a wedding ring. The good Reverend Treat will make us man and wife, and together we'll return to the Indies, where I'll make you princess of any isle you choose."

He never doubted Maria was waiting. He knew from the way she had listened to him that summer, from the way she had loved him, from the way she presented him with a teapot before he set sail. She would be there. But how could he tell her the truth about these last two years?

How could he ask that beautiful, innocent farm girl to marry a pirate?

The treasure hunt had failed. He had found his backer, a forty-year-old Newport goldsmith by the name of Paulsgrave Williams. Together they sailed to the Caribbean. Once there, they realized nearly every sailor in the world had had the same idea. Divers, sent by the king of Spain, the governor of Bermuda, the governor of Jamaica, even the pirate captains Hornigold and Lebous, were all on the search.

While Bellamy's confidence never faltered, supplies were low; he needed more time and money. He never considered returning to New England empty-handed, but the disposition of the crew concerned him. They feared having to return to their lives of near-slavery, an unthinkable fate. Bellamy proposed it, and Williams agreed. The step from treasure hunting to pirating was a small one.

When they asked the men if they wanted to go "on the account," the vote was nearly unanimous. The merchant vessels they had seen regularly since reaching Florida were the sorts of ships on which all of them had been brutally treated. Commandeering them and their cargos would be sweet revenge; the shares they'd take would merely begin to balance the scales of justice. The day they hoisted the skull and crossed bones, Bellamy addressed the crew.

"This flag represents not death," he told them, "but resurrection. Never again will you be captives of the wealthy. From this day, we are new men. Free men."

By January 1716 they had joined forces with Benjamin Hornigold, the veteran. At about the same time, Hornigold was training another new recruit, this one a hulking, intimidating ruffian with a penchant for drama. Dressed in black, he wore a bandolier of crossed pistols across his chest, with still more cutlasses, pistols, and daggers dangling from his belt. When he boarded ships he lit matches and stuck them under his hat, smoke and sparks curling and popping around his head. His long beard hung nearly solid with grease. Drunk, Edward Teach claimed he was the Devil incarnate; others called him Blackbeard.

The students went their own ways, Teach by choice and Bellamy by vote. Hornigold refused to attack English ships, and eventually his crew insisted. Ninety of them, the great majority, voted to oust their captain in favor of Bellamy.

In just over a year since then they had worked the coast, capturing more than fifty ships. Sometimes that meant taking nothing but cargo; often it also meant adding to the crew dissatisfied sailors eager for a taste of independence, and a few others forced to join for their particular talents. When they overtook a larger, newer, or better-constructed ship, the pirates would trade up, or commandeer the vessel, either giving the merchant captain and his men one of their own ships or setting them free on the next one they captured.

It was satisfying work. One morning off Cuba they had taken 28,500 pieces of eight. Last December they captured a vessel that enabled them to make longer voyages, the eighty-foot *Sultana*, with teakwood decks and a gilded poop. After capturing the galley off Saba in the Leeward Islands, the crew had fitted her with fourteen guns.

Then, only two months ago, they had spotted an even larger prize in the Windward Passage. After a three-day chase—he could only admire the nerve of its captain, Lawrence Prince—the one-hundred-foot, three-hundred-ton, three-masted slave ship surrendered peacefully. As the two captains shared a bottle of wine in the captain's cabin, Bellamy learned the *Whydah* had been commissioned as a merchant slaver. Named for the port of Ouida on the West African Slave Coast, the galley was on the final leg of her maiden voyage, carrying ivory, sugar, indigo, and Jesuit's bark.

"Once our cargo is transferred to the *Whydah*," Bellamy had said, "You may have my ship in which to return home."

He could afford to be generous. He had captured the largest ship any pirate had ever commanded. It was in nearly perfect condition and fully provisioned. And the news got better yet. When the boarding party returned, Richard Noland, the quartermaster, reported something Prince had neglected to mention: the *Whydah* also carried gold and silver coins—thousands of them.

The accumulated treasure, evenly divided into sacks, now rested in chests between decks. There was rumbling among the men about quitting; it didn't seem possible they'd get any richer, and piracy was dangerous work.

But this was just the beginning of the riches. To be sure his point was clear to friend and foe, he added cannon and swivel mounts, giving the ship twenty-eight guns, then stripped off the lead sheathing around the hull to increase her speed.

His crew was now divided among three ships: the *Whydah*, the sloop *Mary Ann*, commanded by Williams, and the *Anne*, a 90-ton, two-masted square-rigger commanded by Noland. They had plenty of powder, shot, and provisions, including rum, sugar, molasses, and livestock. Best of all, they had reached New England in time to catch the first of the springtime ships to and from England, which would be well and fully loaded.

Bellamy strode along the deck of the *Whydah* now, his thoughts turning back to this larger problem. It had been easy to convince poor, desperate men to fight for a cause; now that they were wealthy, he had to persuade them anew. He had found himself arguing the point just a fortnight ago, when they had overtaken a sloop out of Boston. He and Williams had been willing to let the merchant captain keep his ship, but the men voted to destroy her. Bellamy took the poor man into his cabin to explain, and to offer him the opportunity to go on the account.

"I'm sorry they won't let you have your sloop again, for I scorn to do anyone a mischief when it is not for my advantage. Damn the sloop, we must sink her, and she might be of use to you."

Captain Beer said, "Surely you and Captain Williams command your crew, and not the other way around? Or perhaps you are no captain at all, but merely a thief obeying your fellow thieves."

Bellamy nearly jumped across the cabin at the man. "Damn you, you are a sneaking puppy—and so are all those who submit to be governed by laws which rich men have made for their own security, for the cowardly whelps have not the courage to defend what they get by their knavery; but damn you altogether." He took Beer by the collar. "Damn them for a pack of crafty rascals, and you, who serve them, for a parcel of hen-hearted numskulls. They vilify us, the scoundrels do, when there is only this difference: they rob the poor under the cover of law, and we plunder the rich under the protection of our own courage. Had you not better make one of us, than sneak after the asses of those villains for employment?"

Captain Beer seemed to give the invitation some thought. After glancing at the broad-chested pirate by the door, seeing no sign that he would be physically assaulted, he answered bravely, if stupidly. "I cannot," he said. "I cannot break the laws of God and man, as you have. You say you're clever, and courageous, but I swear to you now that you'll die by the force of the sea, by the hands of men, or by the hand of God."

"You are a devilish rascal, damn you," Bellamy sneered. "I am a free prince, and I have as much authority to make war on the whole world as he who has a hundred sail of ships at sea, and an army of one hundred thousand men in the field; and this my conscience tells me." He released the man's collar; this shipless captain was beneath disdain.

Beer took the opportunity to speak, but not to beg. "My family is in Newport. If you must sink the sloop, I ask you, by your conscience, set me free."

Bellamy had tried. "Turn him over to Captain Williams," he ordered. "And tell the captain I won't disagree if he chooses to put Captain Beer ashore."

This was what it meant to be free. If some insisted on remaining in cowardly bondage, they deserved the sorry life they chose.

Thomas Davis, a carpenter, took his time replacing a hinge. The hatch closed well enough, if that's all you cared about; but it had enough play that it didn't always come down straight, sometimes catching the edge of the deck. It was dangerous. Besides—though he wouldn't admit this to any of the men around him—he wanted his work done exactly right. He had handsomely outfitted the *Sultana* and, after watching that fine ship sail away, had done as masterful a job in turning the *Whydah* into a man of war. Though he despised the purpose she now served, he had nothing but admiration for the ship and her original builders.

Davis was frustrated. The ship needed serious repairs, more serious than the captain was willing to admit. A few weeks ago they had been caught in a storm they all feared would be their last. The wind seemed to change direction by the minute, and once the sails had been set yards apart Davis had rigged lines and tackle to keep the ship's wheel from spinning out of control, while four men fought to lock the rudder in place. Nonetheless, the main mast step had been sprung, the mast listed, and they had barely attended to it when the stern rail was caved in by a monstrous wave. The ship began taking on a frightening amount of water, even with all pumps manned. Finally, in seawater up to his neck, fighting his fear—like most sailors, he couldn't swim a stroke—Davis found the worst leak. Oakum had spewed out of a seam, and was easily enough replaced.

The step would have to be repaired in port. With the mast supported by splints, the fractured part of the wood socket could be cut away. The numerous smaller leaks in the hull could only be repaired when they careened her in a safe harbor—which was when he and Thomas South hoped to make their escape.

A Welshman, Davis had been the carpenter of a ship called *St. Michael,* sailing from Cork to Jamaica, when she had been captured by Captain Bellamy. Davis had begged for his freedom, something he now knew was a mistake; his crying out was a sign of weakness, something these pirates detested. Among these men it was a point of honor not to lose consciousness when an infected leg or arm was sawn off, or when the wound was seared by a white-hot ax blade. They were traitors, too. One of them had argued, "Damn him, he's a Presbyterian dog, and should fight for King James."

He couldn't entirely blame Bellamy. The ship lacked a carpenter, and as he wasn't married, the crew couldn't see that he had anything to return to. He had asked the captain to promise to set him free with the next vessel they captured, and he had agreed. But when the men learned of the bargain, they put it to a vote, after which one pirate had shouted, "Damn you, we would shoot you or whip you to death at the mast before we'd let you go."

As he finished his work on the hatch, Thomas South, one of his shipmates from the *St. Michael,* came close by. He squatted, his knee touching Davis's.

"Baker has asked me to board the *Mary Anne* with them," the older man said.

Davis immediately opened the hatch again, as if further considering his work. He spoke softly, looking straight ahead as he spoke. "And will you be armed?"

"I've told them I will not," South said.

Both of them considered this. They both knew any hope for eventually returning to an honest life depended on being able to prove they had never thrown their lot in with the pirates.

Just then one of the pirates passed them, spitting in contempt.

South asked loudly, innocently, "Are we sturdy now?"

Davis glanced around and, seeing three of the pirates nearby, answered equally innocently, "Sturdy enough to reach Damaries Cove—and that's what matters, aye?"

The cove, near Richmond Island in southern Maine, was where they would careen. The ship would be unloaded, beached, and turned on her side. Once the hull had dried and been scraped clean of barnacles, the seams would be caulked with tallow and gunpowder to seal leaks. Davis and South planned to escape to one of the nearby wooded islands and await their chance to go to the mainland. According to South, the islands were remote, and fiercely cold even in spring. Davis could scarcely imagine being colder than he was now.

Some days, Bellamy thought later that afternoon, piracy was too easy to be believed.

Just moments ago a sloop had appeared out of the growing fog. The *Whydah* steered close, and now the two were within shouting distance.

"Name yourselves, and from whence you come!" he called.

A short, broad man, hatless, returned, "We are the *Fisher,* from Virginia, bound for Boston." Then, as an afterthought, "We are laden with tobacco and hides."

"And are you her captain?"

The hatless man assented cautiously. "Captain Robert Ingols. And who, might I ask, are you?"

"We are of the sea," Bellamy answered flatly. "Bring your papers and your mate and come aboard." That was the advantage of having twenty-eight cannons and 180 men; it was rarely necessary to fight. He turned and ordered David Turner to send an armed crew to board the *Fisher* and follow the *Whydah*'s light as darkness fell.

Then, curious, Bellamy called back through the cold, damp air, "Are you acquainted with the waters here?"

Captain Ingols answered almost too enthusiastically, clearly hoping for good treatment. "Sir, I know this coast exceedingly well."

Bellamy was glad to hear it. The poor visibility concerned him; the man in the top mast had finally come down, unable to find the darker water of the channel. His pilots, Lambeth and that Indian, Julian, who had been reared on the cape, were first rate, but they were navigating the trickiest coast along the eastern seaboard. To-night, he thought, they would take whatever help they could get.

Above the sails of the flotilla, an Arctic front was descending from the east, northeast, on a collision course with a harbinger of spring:

warm, moist tropical air from the Gulf Stream. Worse, the collision between these air masses was taking place on the very cusp of the polar front, which had begun its annual retreat northward. The closer that front gets to the Arctic Circle, the more unyielding its cold air masses become.

The result of this confrontation would be fog, wind, and rain moving horizontally at sea level, then as the cold front moved closer and drew the air upward, a whipping loop of a storm ripping between the sea and the sky.

Sam Bellamy was sailing into a northeaster.

The rain quickly became blinding. The captured *Mary Anne* lost sight of the lights on the *Whydah*, the *Fisher,* and the *Anne,* lights which now seemed absurdly small and dim to Thomas South, who heard, above the shouts of the men around him, a sound which caught at his heart: the roar of the surf off the lee bow.

"Breakers! Breakers!" voices shouted at once.

Thomas Fitzgerald, the soaking wet nineteen-year-old mate of the *Mary Anne* who was now at the helm, knew he had to force his ship into deeper water. Hearing one of the pirates order the sails trimmed, he hoped desperately the storm hadn't completely thrown off his sense of direction. Unable to see even the length of the deck, it was all he could do to keep a firm grip on the wheel.

The ship never had a chance.

Ferocious winds literally blew through her sails, shredding the cloth; then, amidst the force of the waves, pirates and sailors alike felt a sickening plunge and shudder as the *Mary Anne* ran aground. South saw Baker struggling with the foremast and immediately understood; together they cut it down, then cut the mizzenmast, to lessen the weight on the hull. All the while they worked, waves pounded the side of the crippled ship. Strips of sail and tattered rigging slapped the wood above South's head, and he knew that sound, combined with the smashing of the waves, might be the last he'd ever hear.

"For God's sake," someone yelled against the wind, "let us go down into the hold and die together."

South struggled to follow, but a heavy rope snapped out at his right leg, numbing him with pain as he fell to the deck. He had boarded the cargo ship unarmed, hoping to find freedom, but at this moment he'd gladly swear to sail with anyone who could promise him he'd be alive to see the sun rise. Pulling himself forward with his hands, he reached the ladder and, unable to find his footing on the violently pitching ship, fell into the hold.

Someone closed the hatch.

Empty wine bottles and broken glass rolled as the ship continued to pitch and be smashed by waves, pitch and be smashed. A single lantern threw daggers of light as it swung crazily from a beam. Looking around him, South could see no difference between pirate and sailor, young man or old. There was nothing they could do but huddle here, dripping onto the dirty wood as the waves broke the ship to pieces.

Someone offered him a bottle, and he took it.

"What's that there, young Thomas?" one of the *Mary Anne*'s men called to Fitzgerald.

South looked up and saw that the boy held a book.

The boy answered, miserably, *"The Book of Common Prayer."*

The pirate Baker asked, "Can you read?"

Fitzgerald nodded.

"Then read, damn you."

At that moment a wave hit the ship so hard it blurred Fitzgerald's vision; the men around him shouted out, a mixture of curse and prayer. Then the young man opened the damp book, fumbled for a moment with the pages, and recited from memory:

"Repent ye; for the Kingdom of heaven is at hand."

By now the gale had become a full-scale storm, with winds up to seventy miles an hour and waves thirty to forty feet tall. The three-masted *Whydah* drew a shallow draft for a ship of her size. Top-heavy, she was highly susceptible to the northeasterly winds blowing her closer to the surf line and sandbars.

Bellamy ordered a northerly course on the advice of Ingols, but he quickly lost faith in the sloop's captain who didn't seem to know where he was. As the *Whydah* rose and plunged, Bellamy rushed to the rail and shouted in a booming voice that managed to cut through the storm.

"Noland! Noland!"

The quartermaster came to the rail of the *Anne,* which rode close by the *Whydah.*

"Bring Montgomery forth!" Bellamy's order was nearly overwhelmed by a rumble of thunder, but he saw the *Anne*'s captain come forward. Holding fast, Bellamy shouted, "Guide us to Cape Cod Harbor—" his ship seemed to disappear beneath him, followed a moment later by the *Anne,* "—Guide us to Cape Cod Harbor and earn your freedom and your ship!"

The man didn't respond.

Nearly hurling his body forward with the force of his voice, Bellamy repeated, with anger vented at the elements, "Your freedom and your ship!"

Noland turned to his prisoner and said, "She's yours to save."

Montgomery wasted no time in moving to the wheel; he hadn't brought his ship this far to have it wrecked by thieves. He took with him to the helm his cook, a veteran seaman on his last journey—a man he trusted.

"Turn us west, northwest."

"Sir?" the cook repeated, both hands on the wheel. He assumed he had misheard.

"Damn these devils," Montgomery answered, "do you think they'd keep their promise? Run us toward shore. The moment you see the galley run aground, head out to sea."

"Damn the gods!" Bellamy thundered, staring up at the sky. "Damn the devils of the sea!" Hearing the breakers growling to his lee, he knew he had been betrayed.

Eyes flashing to rival the lightning, Bellamy turned to his faithful men. "Do exactly as I say! Drop the bow anchor!" Though the wind was against him, he would try to conjure it into pushing him away from shore. First, he needed to pivot the *Whydah.*

He heard the order repeated and followed with remarkable speed. His crew could barely balance on the heaving deck as they lowered the half-ton anchor and fathom after fathom of heavy iron chain into the angry foam. Almost before the flukes could have reached bottom, he sensed it; a moment later he knew. It wouldn't hold.

"Drop the lee anchor!" he shouted into the rain blown nearly horizontal, the sheets of spray and crests of waves crashing onto the decks. A wave caught Julian and Lambert, still by the wheel, and hurled them into the netting.

The men dropped the second anchor, cable whipping past at life-threatening speed, taking skin and fingers as it went.

Bellamy roared to his pilots, still regaining their feet, "When the ship meets the wind, tack southwest!"

"Southwest!" Julian repeated.

The combined weight of the anchors held the ship in place, momentarily—and that may have been the worst thing that happened. As she strained against the cable, immobile, unable to ride the waves, the waves began to hammer the *Whydah* mercilessly.

Nevertheless, frightened men fought to set the sails, struggling to climb the soaked rigging as it froze and snapped. As Bellamy watched, an enormous wave caught him unprepared, and as he fell to his knees two of the men were blown screaming into the bottomless gulf beneath them. Even as others scurried to take their places, the wind punched holes in the sails, holes that immediately grew, canvas flapping in the wind.

Dragging anchor, the ship drifted closer to the shoals. As this happened, the men slashed at the canvas they had just rigged to slow their windblown progress toward shore.

"Cut the anchor cable!" Bellamy roared, and when no one seemed to respond, rushed to do the job himself.

The crew had heard him—but severing the cable was a gamble with death, leaving them completely at the storm's mercy. Wielding axes, they joined him in desperation, chopping at the cable until it snapped free. Feet planted on the deck, Bellamy ordered a small sail set, hoping that a miraculous change in the direction of the wind might blow them to deeper water.

His hope lasted less than a minute.

That's how long it took for the *Whydah* to run hard aground, stern first, knocking some men to their knees and others into the sea. Towering waves immediately began pummeling the impaled ship. As she began to list at an angle nearly impossible to climb, much less walk, men scrambled to get below decks even as their mates were washed to their death or crushed. Bellamy, holding to the rigging, saw a solitary figure actually trying to cross the deck, an act of lunacy.

And if Thomas Davis had been given a moment to think, he no doubt would have admitted his plan was crazy. But in the chaos of the tempest, tripping over snapped lines and torn sails, face whipped to bleeding by a scrap of his shirt, he believed that if only he could free the ship of her masts, she might float free of the bar.

Before he even reached the damaged mainmast, it fell with a crash that shook more men to their deaths. Davis shoved his arms through a gunport to keep from plunging overboard, and it wasn't until a wave slammed his teeth into his own handiwork that he realized he had dropped his saw. The splintering decks and cracking spars were repair jobs he would never finish—but what brought him to his senses was the sight of iron rods bent like melted candles. Braver men than he were screaming for their lives, crying, calling to the gods for help. He could see that he had as much chance of reaching the ladder, now nearly above him, as he had of leaping to the moon; but beneath him the nightmarish sea was obvious death. Turning, he thought to wait for the next wave to pass, then make his best effort for the ladder.

Thomas Davis did not understand the weight of water. When the wave he thought he would ride out came, a force of several tons collapsed onto him from twenty feet over his head, flipping him overboard as easily as a sledgehammer flattens an egg.

Breaker after breaker rose from the ocean, reaching high enough to rip down men who had climbed into the rigging in a vain attempt to escape. Bellamy somehow managed to keep his hold, clutching one of the remaining masts, though at one point he looked down to find that the rushing water had sucked the shoes and socks from his feet. At that strange sight he felt oddly elated; then he realized the buoyancy he felt was the ship itself, bobbing free.

The *Whydah* galley rose just long enough to take a mountainous wave against her hull; as she capsized, the storm broke her back with an agonizing crack. Cannons tore free from their mounts, knocking out support beams and crashing through the decks, followed by tons of shot, casks of nails, water, and salt beef, chickens, cows—and over 180 bags of equally divided silver, gold, and jewels, carefully packed in chests—all of which crushed the pirates who had survived thus far, breaking their bones, drowning them and, moments later, anchoring them to the ocean floor.

Two lived.

One was the Indian pilot, John Julian, who wandered the shore aimlessly. Three months later he was in a Boston prison; after that, he disappeared into the mist of unrecorded history.

The other man was sure he had frozen to death even as he clung to a piece of wreckage. In later years he would have no memory of the time that passed between being swept from the ship and feeling the sand beneath his feet, perhaps because he had been unconscious, but also because the trip to shore took barely more than three minutes. Sixty seconds more in the water, which was below forty degrees that night, and he could not have survived.

In any event, when Thomas Davis felt bottom he immediately tried to stand, and when the surf tugged him back toward the ocean he fought with all his remaining strength. The water was hip deep, then knee deep—he fell, sinking his hands into the sand and shells, but this time a wave actually pushed him forward—and when he had crawled to water that just washed over the backs of his bleeding hands, he stopped to thank God. Truly, this was a miracle. No man could have survived such a wreck without the divine guidance of the Almighty. Barely able to believe his good fortune, he raised his head to give thanks—

—and saw, extending into the darkness on either side, a hundred foot cliff.

Davis cursed.

The forty-degree temperature driven lower by ferocious winds was every bit as life-threatening on land as it had been at sea. He turned to see the capsized hull, briefly illuminated by lightning, but heard not a single shout. Realizing the impossibility of remaining in the water, he did the only sensible thing: he began to climb.

To a man who had climbed ship's rigging in high winds, the white cliff was not an insurmountable challenge—but Davis was drenched and freezing, his right forefinger seemed to be broken, and whatever was wrong with his left ankle, he could put no weight on it. So he made his way slowly, pulling himself up handhold by handhold, the still-raging storm forcing him against the wall, chilling him, at the same time sending rain running down his face. When it ran into his mouth, it gave him pause; then he recognized the taste of fresh water.

Encouraged, he pulled himself higher, heart skipping each time a hand slid, forcing himself to reach upward ten times before pausing, then ten more. Beneath him the waves crashed, and it seemed impossible that the same ocean people traveled and fished every day had been deep and strong enough to kill over one hundred of the strongest men he had ever known.

He promised himself a rest at the top of the cliff, but once there he felt surprisingly rejuvenated. Slowed by the fog and darkness, he began limping through tall grasses in the only direction that concerned him: away from the sea. If he had altered his course by less than a hundred yards, he would have found himself at a simple hut where Maria Hallett lay awake, listening to the storm; instead he stumbled blindly ahead for the better part of an hour until, exhausted, he collapsed.

A few hours later he awoke, hungry, stiff, and cold. Face nearly frozen, he lay in soaking, sandy grass, momentarily confused. Then memory returned, supported by the evidence of his misery. Trying to stand, he spotted a fallen tree limb that would serve as a crutch. He then set out in a light rain he barely noticed, for rain had become a constant condition of the world, as imperceptible as nitrogen in the air, or sand in the soil. Though he had no way of knowing, it was five o'clock in the morning, and he had walked a total of two miles when he spotted the farmhouse.

Hobbling toward his first sign of civilization, he hammered the door with his hands, pounding urgently against the wood.

The farmer, Samuel Harding, was less than delighted to be awakened.

"Who might you be?" he gruffly asked the stranger.

Thomas Davis could only weep.

From his visitor's appearance, Harding knew the young man had been the victim of miserable misfortune. He took him by the arm and led him inside.

When Davis could speak, he told the farmer, "I am cast ashore from a shipwreck so furious only God in his anger at human folly could have caused it. I do not know for sure, but I believe I am the only survivor. The screams of the men around me were the last I heard of them."

In keeping with the cape's tradition of succor to shipwreck survivors, Harding asked no further questions for the moment. "Come, warm yourself by the fire. We'll give you some tea."

Davis continued to be amazed—at the existence of a dry room, a fire, a teapot. It hardly seemed imaginable that he had returned to this world. As he dried, he felt overcome by gratitude toward the man and woman across from him. In exchange for their kindness, he told them a story of capture on the high seas, of piracy and bloodshed, of treasure these good people never could have imagined.

Harding and his wife listened silently for over an hour. While it was the unlikeliest tale they had ever heard, there was no doubting a word this young man spoke.

"Black Bellamy certainly got what fate he deserved," Harding said when the story was finished. "Acquiring riches by force is a sin against man and God."

Davis concurred; Harding's wife nodded. And then the three of them shared the same thought.

"Do you suppose," Harding asked, "there is anything left to salvage?"

CAPE COD

THERE HAS ALWAYS BEEN A sense of adventure in our family. My father and my Uncles Rolly and Bill all fought in World War II. I grew up listening to the three of them sitting around a woodstove in a cabin in Maine telling the kinds of stories men like that tell, stories about hunting, fishing, and women.

And treasure.

My grandfather, a one-time boxer, fought in World War I and later joined the Merchant Marine. While he was in Africa in the mid-forties he bought diamonds, as an investment, but before he got them home, he died at sea. My grandmother—a wonderful, spirited woman who once dated Wallace Beery and many years later, when she was in her mid-eighties, demanded to go diving with me—hired a detective to find them, but they never turned up. That pretty much started the whole family treasure hunting.

The rest of them eventually gave the diamonds up for lost. Since then, I've learned that while people who don't believe a particular treasure exists can be hard to persuade, the real opposition to treasure hunters comes from the people who believe it exists and aren't willing to do the work—or spend the money—to find it. I can remember my father laughing at Bill when he talked about the *Whydah.*

Bill was the sort of man who worried other adults—my parents, for instance—for the very good reason that he seemed to be having a wonderful adventure nearly every day of his life. As far as they were concerned, that could only make him a dangerous influence on a child, especially if that child was me.

"There hasn't been any treasure out there since a week after the wreck," my father would say. "You'd be lucky to find a few old nails."

"You never heard of anybody coming up with thirty thousand pounds of coins," Bill said. "Those twenty-eight cannons didn't wash ashore."

Rolly laughed at both of them. "Even if there *was* that kind of money on board—which I don't believe there was—it's dribbled away. Picked up here and there. That fellow Seth Knowles says he got nearly six hundred pieces of eight. Add up all the people who have a few old coins, then multiply by two hundred and fifty years."

That's when Bill would say: "Gold don't float."

They had answers for that, too, the same answers everyone had. Some said Paulsgrave Williams came back and lifted the treasure off the wreck; some said the reports of the ship's riches were just good stories, and should be appreciated as such, especially considering how pirates liked to enhance their reputations. People who had given the matter a little more thought pointed out that the *Whydah* had gone down in relatively shallow water; for years there were reported sightings of her hull during unusually low tides, offering plenty of salvaging opportunities to anyone who didn't mind getting his feet wet.

"It's still down there," Bill insisted. "And that hull people saw, that wasn't her."

"What makes you so sure?" my father said. "Are you some kind of reincarnated pirate?"

"Yo ho ho," Rolly said.

"You'll see," Uncle Bill would tell them. "Ask Jack Poole. He dove for it. Some day somebody's going to go after that ship the right way and come up a millionaire."

"What's that to you? You're already a millionaire."

The truth was, Bill had done well in cape real estate, though you'd never guess it to look at him. About all he ever wore was a plaid shirt, blue jeans, and moccasins, the jeans cuffed so he could tap his cigarette ashes into them. When he was fifteen he too ran off to join the Merchant Marine. From Hawaii he sent his mother a photograph of a native girl in a grass skirt and a letter asking for $500 so they could get married. She didn't send the money, and he never did get married. Back on the cape, he once led a cow into the Presbyterian Church belfry on a Saturday night just to rattle the congregation the next morning. He lived with my grandmother in a big old house in Brewster where he read *Argosy* and adventure magazines, getting out to hunt and fish at every opportunity.

During the 1950s, when I spent summers on the cape, it was still wild and desolate, inhabited mostly by deer, rabbits, minks, muskrats, ducks, and pheasants. My family stayed on Robbins Hill, which Uncle Rolly and Aunt Marilyn practically owned. The rich people, city people, stayed in town; when some of them wanted to buy Rolly's land, he sold it cheap, laughing the whole time: what kind of fool would want to live on a cold, windy hill? You know the rest of the story. In ten years it was all being developed, and the city slickers had the last laugh. Rolly and Marilyn kept only a small cottage for themselves, where twelve of us lived in the summers. The cottage overlooked beautiful sand flats, and at low tide we'd walk out to the breakers nearly a mile away. Families would drive down to the flats in their bug-eyed Buicks and high-finned Plymouths to watch the sunset.

We spent most of our time outdoors, where my father taught me how to survive on the sea and in the woods. The lessons Bill taught had more to do with attitude. He was a champion braggart when it came to fishing, but he was lucky, too; just when my father and Rolly thought they had him caught in a hopeless lie about one fishing spot or another, he'd come in with the evidence. Bill seemed to enjoy getting himself into difficult situations. He'd keep rolling the dice, taking risks.

Where Bill had fun, my father had regrets. He had dreamed of being a major league baseball player, and he might have made it. Six foot two, big and muscular, he looked like a stronger Ted Williams. Like Williams, his plans were interrupted by World War II, when he left Boston University to serve his country. After the war he married my mother and chose to do the responsible thing: settle down, raise a family. My father sold insurance and real estate; my mother was in real estate before becoming a nurse. They are both honest, hardworking people. But what does honest and hard-working mean to a boy? As much as I admired my father, there was no question who I wanted to imitate.

Uncle Bill's example was one of the reasons I got into trouble as a kid. I wasn't doing anything serious, just mischief really—whatever I could do that would get somebody to chase me through the woods. Sometimes I think I did things just to try to scare myself, to see how far I'd go.

When I was twelve years old I told my parents I wanted a car. I was at least as strong-willed then as I am now, and eventually they got me a '51 Studebaker. Using leftover house paint, I painted the Studebaker brown with white flames. I'd sit in school, barely paying attention (in the space at the bottom of my report cards, where there was room for a note to the parents, my teachers were always writing, "Barry is a daydreamer"), and the minute I got home I'd whistle for Rocky, my black lab (named for Rocky Marciano, the boxer). Then I'd wrestle my Old Town canoe onto the roof, grab my double barreled shotgun, and Rocky and I would make the half-mile drive to the cranberry bogs.

I had a trapline, where I caught mink and muskrat, and now and then Rocky and I would bring my mother a pheasant. But as much time as I spent hunting, I spent at least as much exploring. I still remember the sweet perfume of wild roses, honeysuckle, and beach plums. One of my favorite places was a big split rock I was sure had been an Indian site. Rocky and I found arrowheads around it, and while he kept looking I'd scramble to the top of the rock and just sit there, looking out over the water. It hardly took any imagination at all for a twelve-year-old boy to see pirates sailing around the bend in the cove.

When I finally told someone else what I daydreamed about those long afternoons, I said it with the kind of confidence that still gets me into trouble.

It was after our last high school football game. A bunch of buddies and I went exploring around Wellfleet, and we ended up at the beach. Even though it was nearly three in the morning, the moon was just rising—the biggest, most perfectly formed moon I'd ever seen, creating a path of light leading out across the water. The ocean seemed to come alive; if there were ever ghosts, they were all walking around that night.

I said, "There's a shipwreck loaded with gold out there, and I'm going to find it."

We were riding high; that night, everything seemed possible. But finding the *Whydah* would take a lot more than a moonbeam and a teenager's wishful thinking.

Though I didn't realize it then, everything I did after that night prepared me to track down Bellamy's flagship.

I had always spent as much time as I could on or near the water. After graduating from high school, and during summers home from college, I taught swimming and canoeing at a Boy Scout camp, and I was the head lifeguard at Dennis Beach. That was my first job that involved life and death responsibilities. Ironically, the one time I may have saved someone's life came on my day off.

One day on the cape I had strapped an air tank on my back, dove into a pond, and swam across and back under water. It was my first dive. With all the swimming I did, diving came easily; I didn't take a class, didn't even get certified until years later. This was before scuba classes were easily accessible. In retrospect, it seems a foolish thing to have tried on my own. After that, when I wasn't lifeguarding I put my tank on and went to a place where I had good luck finding lobsters. I had to pass some private property to get there, so I'd dive, swim down to the spot, spear some fish, then leave when the tide changed.

This one afternoon I had caught a couple of lobsters and a half dozen flounder when I surfaced long enough to have a look around. I heard someone shouting; glancing toward the beach, I saw a young woman standing, shading her eyes, looking past me. As I turned I heard it again, a boy's voice: "It's got me!"

Instinctively, I thought shark. I dropped my catch, my tank, and my weight belt, then swam, still wearing my fins, carrying my spear gun, in the direction of the voice.

It took me a minute to find the kid; even though the tide was on its way out, and I swam hard, he was two or three hundred yards offshore, and when I called to him he just kept screaming. When I saw his head, I swam a few strokes closer, then did a surface dive.

I saw something long and thin, but it wasn't a shark; the boy had shot himself with his own spear gun, pinning his legs together, and the tide was carrying him out to sea.

Back on the surface, I told him to calm down, got a hold on him, and started toward the shore. The girl I had seen, who turned out to be his sister, kept screaming. Before we reached her, I was able to hail a fishing boat and get the boy to the hospital. The next night his parents came to the restaurant where I worked part time, told me he was going to be all right, and gave me a sweater. It felt great to have gotten the job done when it mattered.

I kept going to school, dutifully, but without much interest in classes. In 1965 I entered Colorado's Trinidad Junior College on a football scholarship. Trinidad was an outlaw school, a place athletes went to learn big league tactics and improve their grades. People used to say that if you could start at Trinidad, you could play anywhere. I'm not sure that's true, but it was one of the wildest places I'd ever been. The college had a large gunsmithing school, so school rules made it perfectly acceptable to carry guns. On any given day the cafeteria tables would be covered with pistols scattered among the plates of roast beef and gravy.

At the time I started college, a lot of guys were just returning from Vietnam. It seemed the average age for freshmen was twenty-five. I got there thinking I was pretty tough, but to them I was this kid from a little prep school in Maine who showed up at the bus station in Trinidad wearing a pair of Bass Weejuns. I had a lot to prove.

As a condition of my football scholarship I served as a dorm counselor, which meant, among other things, breaking up fights. I was nearly stabbed by a guy on my hall one night, but he was drunk enough that I was able to wrap a towel around my arm, knock the knife away, drag him to his room, and put him to bed. After that I was more attentive. That's how I met Rob McClung.

Early one term I was sitting in a history class, only half paying attention, when I noticed this guy who was about average height, maybe a little shorter. He looked like Yul Brynner, with that square jaw, deep-set brown eyes, and high cheek bones. In some weird show of freshman arrogance, he had made the mistake of wearing his karate black belt to class. The ballplayers at Trinidad were real badasses, the wrong guys to show off around. But what caught my attention was that he was obviously boiling with anger. The whole time the history teacher rambled on, this guy practiced his karate, breaking pencils with his finger.

At that time Rob weighed about a hundred and forty-five pounds. After leaving Florida State he went to Trinidad, where his grandfather owned the newspaper. It's an understatement to say Rob didn't want to be there. In Florida he had been the state diving champion and an all-around star athlete; here he was lost in the shuffle.

I talked to him after class, and soon he was telling me about rambles through the Everglades that sounded a lot like my explorations of the cape. He was obsessed with getting stronger, so I introduced him to weight lifting. More than just an athlete, Rob had a talent for crazy stunts. Once he did a handstand on top of a flagpole; another time he dove from a railroad bridge, through high tension wires, to the water seventy-five feet below. Once I made the mistake of double-dating with him; he tried to impress the girls we were with by jumping off a cliff into the tops of the trees.

At the end of the year we transferred to Western State in Gunnison, Colorado, where we played football, skied, climbed mountains, and poked through abandoned gold-rush towns. We kept testing ourselves; one time we floated the Purgatory River in cutoffs, barefoot, carrying nothing but our knives. We felt invincible, bulletproof.

Even back then, I noticed that Rob was different when it wasn't just the two of us. When we were alone, we had great times together, and he seemed comfortable being himself. When there were others around, though, he kept trying to take charge. It irritated some of the others, but they didn't often say anything: by that time Rob was even more physically intimidating, thanks to the weight lifting, and he had an imposing attitude.

One of the friends we made was Trip Wheeler, who I first saw when I looked out my window to find out what all the yelling was about. A guy with long blond hair and cowboy boots, wearing jeans but no shirt, was going down the street on a motorcycle—standing. He had looks the girls loved; some of them had a contest to see who could climb to the window of his room the fastest. Trip's claim to fame, though, is in Crested Butte. He threw himself, or got thrown, through the front window of Oscar's Grub Stake saloon so many times that the owners finally named it after him. You can still get people telling stories by walking into Oscar's ordering a beer, and asking about Trip.

One of the other students I got to know was a beautiful girl, a champion skier. We spent long, idyllic days together, skiing and wandering the hills and making plans. Soon enough, we were crazy with love. When Patsy found out she was pregnant we got married, her all of nineteen and me twenty-two. Not long after our son, Barry Jr., was born, we learned that Patsy was pregnant again.

It was a wild time and a wild life for us. I guess finally we were too much for each other, and too young. We separated and, after some failed attempts at reconciliation, divorced.

I had graduated from Gunnison with a double major in history and sociology and a minor in physical education. I volunteered for Navy flight school, but my chances ended when they learned I was color blind. After the divorce, Patsy headed off to South America; Barry Jr. and Jenny, our baby, remained with me.

That was a terrible time; after finding a wonderful relationship, it had all gone wrong. I was twenty-seven, didn't want to date anybody, could barely stand to talk to anybody; my priority was to raise Jenny and Barry somewhere safe, protected. I thought of Martha's Vineyard, which reminded me of what the cape had been when I was growing up: beautiful and unspoiled. I packed up the kids and moved.

Rob McClung came east, too, and together we took jobs as administrators for the Boy Scouts of America. They were looking for athletes at the time, the pay wasn't bad, and they gave me a car to use. I made a down payment on a house and built a stone wall around it, in part for privacy, in part as therapy. It was a relief to concentrate on the physical act of carrying stones, fitting them together. When I was finished I dug a pond, then built a boat. After a year I left the Boy Scouts for a job teaching phys. ed. at Bourne High School on the cape. As a football coach I built obstacle courses for the kids, getting them to test themselves, to overcome their self-imposed limitations.

Jenny and Barry went everywhere with me. Jenny used to stand behind me in the Jeep, her arms around my neck, while Barry Jr. slept in the passenger seat. Baby-sitting help came from an unlikely source. One of my high school students, Carl Rokoff, was a troubled kid, wild, somebody the other teachers hated to deal with—one day he was led out of the building in handcuffs. He reminded me of me. He was adopted, and resented it. When I met him, Carl was having some disagreements with the police concerning his collection of other people's sportscars. When I left teaching and used my construction skills to make a living, I hired him as a carpenter. One thing I learned teaching swimming, then coaching football, was that if you give people challenges, and reward them when they meet those challenges, they can accomplish some amazing things. That was certainly true for Carl; he was great with the kids.

I saw a few women while I lived on the Vineyard, but my heart was still torn. On top of my confusion following the divorce, the Vineyard was changing. Once a place where people cultivated vegetable gardens and heated their homes with woodstoves, it was being taken over by people who brought drugs and BMWs. I wasn't interested in the new trust-fund crowd, and the truth is, I was starting to get restless.

In 1972 I hired a beautiful young Swedish woman to come paint murals in the kids' rooms. Birgitta was calm and kind and talented. We quickly found ourselves becoming involved. Jenny and Barry loved her. By the time she finished painting she felt like a part of our lives; she moved in as nurturer and keeper of the household. Looking back, I don't know what we would have done without her.

I felt like the proverbial new man, finally able to pick up the other part of my life where I had left off. Having a tank and a wet suit meant I could supplement my income doing small salvaging jobs: pulling nets from the wheels of fishing boats, raising small anchors and boats, inspecting the bottoms of ships for insurance claims—that sort of thing. I even did a little underwater surveying. After Birgitta moved in, I started diving on local wrecks, just for my own enjoyment. I'd do as much research as I could on a ship and the circumstances of the wreck, and learned that if I did the work carefully I'd usually find what I was after. That was the pleasure of it: searching for something old and forgotten. I dove on dozens of wrecks, and once in a while I'd discover a bottle, a piece of china, or even an old ship's bell.

I started doing more dangerous jobs, jobs that paid a lot. That's why I did them, and I usually did them alone. I liked the money and I had confidence and was very careful. Soon I was working for a tugboat captain who had been hired to raise a ship's propeller from a turn-of-the-century merchant vessel that had gone down near Cuttyhunk. The men who hired him had tried to raise the propeller themselves, but couldn't; my boss tried and failed, and when I said I knew how to do it, he dared me to try.

Jenny and Barry were in school by then. Thanks to them I met John Beyer, who was dating one of their teachers. He seemed like a nice enough guy, easygoing and friendly, and as we talked I got the impression he was looking for work. He said the salvaging I did sounded interesting; I asked him if he had done any diving. When he said yes, I told him I could use some help.

Understand, this was work, not recreation; the propeller everyone was trying to raise, eighteen feet in diameter, weighed twelve and a half tons, and lay in deep water. Four of us were going to dive in pairs; since John was the unknown quantity, I teamed up with him. I was standing on the deck in my Uni suit—a dry suit with hood and booties attached, the sort of suit you need when you dive in cold water day after day—and I was checking my air pressure when John lifted his tanks. He did it like an Englishman trying to swing a baseball bat. I watched him a moment longer just to make sure.

"So," I said, "you've done a lot of diving."

John fumbled with a strap. "Not a lot."

"But you've done some deep stuff, right?" I enjoy adventure, but recklessness is something else. I had no interest in diving with somebody whose inexperience might get both of us in trouble.

"I used to be a photographer for hotel brochures," he said. "They'd want pictures of people swimming and diving, so I did some underwater shots."

"You're telling me you've been diving in swimming pools?"

John stammered.

"Look," I said. "You may not be a diver, but I can't afford to waste a day. Remember two things: Don't hold your breath, and do what I tell you to do. Got it?" He nodded, and with that we went over the side.

Beyer has bright blue eyes; as we went down the line they kept getting bigger and bigger. The propeller was at 110 feet, and to get to it we had to swim under the starboard side of the listing ship. At that depth in northern waters there's barely any light, just enough to reveal the silt suspended in the water. When we looked up we saw a wall of black with things dangling down, all sorts of growth from the side of the ship reaching out at us—imagine long lengths of furry intestines swaying over your head. At the bottom we sank into mud up to our necks.

Beyer just hung on, staring blindly, trying not to look up, or around, or anywhere—he was in a scene from a nightmare. I tapped his arm to remind him: *keep breathing.* He nodded, then worked up the nerve to let go of the guide line. And he came through. Working in shifts, the four of us wrapped the propeller in metal cables so it could be lifted by a rented crane on a 100-foot barge. We had it out of the water by the end of the afternoon.

I get grief for that propeller to this day. My boss, the tugboat captain, claimed I "stole" the job from him, and the people who had hired him wrote letters to the local paper calling me a pirate. That's when I learned that everyone in the salvage business gets a bad reputation. If you can't find or raise what you go after, you're a failure; if you do raise it, there are plenty of people who hate you for getting what they wanted.

That was only the beginning.

On March 19, 1979, one of the Martha's Vineyard ferries, the *Islander,* was leaving Oak Bluffs on the crossing to Woods Hole on the cape when she struck a rock about a quarter of a mile out. The captain tried to return to the dock, but the ferry was taking on too much water; he lost his ability to maneuver and hit the pilings. No one was hurt, and they managed to unload the cars and passengers using a special ramp. Although the water was only twenty feet deep, the ship was still in danger of sinking, and before it could float, someone had to patch the hole.

When I reached the scene, there were only a few other divers, none of them with any salvaging experience. Since I always carried my gear in the Jeep, when I saw what was going on I put on my Uni suit and fins (I tried not to wear gloves, preferring the dexterity of bare fingers), dove in—and nearly froze. I later found out the water was about as cold as it had been the night the *Whydah* sank. Even with my dry suit on, I thought I was about to go hypothermic.

The *Islander* had four holes in her starboard side and a sixty-foot crack running down her center. After the inspection, I told the people from the Steamship Authority that ran the ferries what I thought should be done to make the boat tight again, then set about doing it. The job involved stretching a tarpaulin over the holes to stem the flow of water, installing plywood and foam patches to the outside of the hull, applying plywood patches on the inside, then covering those with steel patches.

The work would have been complicated under any circumstances. Given the water temperature, the fact that I worked and supervised shifts of divers around the clock for thirty-six hours, and the position of the ship, it was the most dangerous job I had ever taken on. A storm was blowing up, and the hull kept rising from the seabed, then dropping like a giant cleaver. If I had been even momentarily careless, someone could have been crushed. And the whole time we worked on repairing the holes we were being sucked up into the ship—we had to work just to stay in place. Diving through the decks, swimming through the corridors lit by underwater lamps, knowing firemen and Coast Guard officers waited at the surface, I felt like a character in a disaster movie.

At some point late that night I realized the job was going to be worth a lot of money, and I knew what I wanted to do with it. The rest of the time I swam in and around the *Islander*, I kept thinking of salvaging Bellamy's ship.

But they didn't pay me.

Alfred Ferro, a representative of the Steamship Authority, told newspaper reporters the next day that everyone who had worked on the ship "did one hell of a job." When it came time to write the check, though, the Steamship Authority said they thought I had been donating my services. I made what may have been perceived as an impolite comment about their mental stability. Then they said the other divers had charged less. I had planned and supervised the repairs, and had done a lot of the work myself under that bobbing hull, but they thought if they kept arguing they would eventually save money.

So I called my lawyer, Allan Tufankjian. Allan and I have been friends since grade school, and when I asked him to check federal admiralty laws he knew exactly what I was up to. It turned out that I was right: salvage law flatly stated that I could claim salvage rights to the ferry. Furthermore, if the Steamship Authority refused to pay me, I could bring proceedings to have the court establish the amount due me for salvage claim.

You can imagine how that went over. During the trial the Authority indicated it would be willing to pay me my standard hourly wage, that would have come to a grand total of slightly under $3,000. Not good enough for risking my life.

It took four years for a federal judge to award me $150,000, another four years to win three appeals and finally get approximately $50,000 in interest and costs. I won more than money. Circuit Judge Selya wrote in his decision on the case, "We revisit . . . the subaqueous exploits of plaintiff-appellant Barry Clifford, a highly skilled diver who, under difficult and dangerous conditions, effected emergency repairs to the ferry *M/V Islander* after she was holed." As much of a headache as that job caused, it served as a good experience. If the sharks don't get you, their lawyers will. I was fortunate to have my friend Allan representing me.

I thought I had it all. Diving was going well. I was making money and I hadn't gotten hurt. (But I knew it would only be a matter of time before Mother Nature caught up with me. No one lasts long in the diving business without getting hurt.) At the same time, Birgitta and I had a son, Brandon, and she and I were married on the island. Life was wonderful. Birgitta was a stabilizing influence. While she and I didn't roam the countryside, we shared what I now realize were some of the best years of my life.

But no matter how hard Birgitta tried to keep me inside the walls of our property on the Vineyard, I was constantly drawn to the sea. I'd catch myself staring out the windows, feeling like a schoolboy in late May. I understood and respected my parents, and admired what it took to raise a family, to nurture children. But I couldn't change no matter how hard I tried.

. . .

After Bill was diagnosed with lung cancer, I made time to be with him. He wanted to see some of his favorite places, so we drove up the coast to Maine. Along the way he talked, but without mentioning his illness, although some days he was so sick he could barely walk. Listening to him, I came to some decisions about how I wanted to live, and what I wanted to accomplish. Watching him, I was convinced it would be a mistake to wait any longer.

When he talked about shipwrecks, I asked him whether Jack Poole's coins were really from the *Whydah*.

"A lot of money wrecks off the cape, Boy." He called everyone Boy.

"I want to go after her."

"Don't waste your time."

That was Bill all over; he would antagonize you. Say it was good weather for April and he'd argue last April had been better; say the sky was bright blue and he'd tell you it was white. It was his way of making conversation.

"I'm going to find her."

He had been looking out the car window. When he turned to me it was just for a moment, to make sure I heard him; then he looked back out at the ocean.

He said: "You'll never find her."

"You watch me," I told him.

Then he looked at me and grinned, showing the gap between his front teeth. "You'll never know unless you try, Boy."

At the end of that last drive, Bill gave me his old Indian head ring, which I still wear. When Bill died, in 1982, I lost a great friend. Some days I look at his ring and wish he could have stayed around long enough to see everything that happened, the good and bad, once I set my mind to the hunt.

HUNTING DOWN THE WHYDAH

I CAN'T POINT TO ONE particular day on the calendar. From the diving I had done solely for the pleasure of identifying old wrecks, I knew a lot of the work—sometimes the majority—had to be done on land, and was as physically demanding as browsing through a library's card catalog. Beginning in the late seventies, I devoted a lot of my spare time to reading about the *Whydah,* learning more about the history of the cape, collecting old maps and charts, and seeing just how much useful, reliable information was out there. By the summer of 1982, all the research and conversation and daydreaming that had been simmering in my subconscious started to boil; I realized that if I could get the answers to only a few more questions, I could make a serious stab at finding Bellamy's ship.

One of the attractive aspects of treasure hunting is that there's no job application. You pursue it on your own, and unless your successes or failures are spectacular, no one pays much attention. A lot of people do some kind of hunting—nosing around, really—in their free time. The difference between those people and true treasure hunters is that treasure hunters are willing to quit their jobs and put whatever they've saved into the hunt. The next step comes when you're onto something so big that you've got to convince other people to make the same kinds of sacrifices. Sitting at my desk after dinner that summer, I knew I was ready.

. . .

In the five years I had spent seriously researching the history of the *Whydah,* I came to believe three things:

So many legends evolved concerning Bellamy and his ship because it's easier to create a legend than it is to discover the truth.

The treasure was still out there, more or less where it had fallen two hundred and sixty-five years ago.

In the twentieth century, only one person had made a serious attempt to find it.

If you look at a map, the cape sticks out from the eastern seaboard like a seventy-mile-long hook—or like the arm of a ninety-seven pound weakling trying to flex his bicep. It was formed by glaciers retreating north during one of the last ice ages, and the fist at the top has seemed to shake at sailors ever since. The intrusion of land into the sea, coupled with paralyzing coastal fogs and northeasters—wicked storms packing gale force winds that kick up and shift direction, then shift again—has caused over two thousand shipwrecks, earning the cape its nickname: the Graveyard of the Atlantic.

Cape Cod was an isolated place in Maria Hallett's day. The only road, referred to by locals as the King's Highway, was a narrow dirt track that followed the old trail of the Nauset Indians along the dunes. Most people came by boat, but the fact is, not many people came. Bostonians were the only ones close enough to go to the trouble, and even they didn't have much reason. The cape was the home of sailors, smugglers, and fishermen—a rough crowd—as well as farmers and their families. In the eighteenth century most Americans were trying to find protection from nature, not a way to get back to it. The earliest form of tourism didn't start until after the Civil War, and until the introduction of Route 6 in the 1960's, travel to and on the cape was enough of a nuisance to keep most visitors away—which was just fine with the people who lived here.

There's another perverse thing about Cape Codders: despite the fact that nearly all of them spend time at sea for one reason or another, nothing excites them more—from sailor to lobsterman to constable to reverend—than news of a shipwreck.

Imagine commuters watching eagerly for a ten-car pileup, airplane pilots delighted to hear a 747 has gone down. Schoolboys who stared out the windows in those days weren't idly dreaming; they were hoping to see a ship in distress. When they saw one, they rushed from the classroom without bothering to be excused, their teachers hot on their heels.

Shipwrecks were the country's earliest lottery. Instead of playing a number, you simply went about your daily work hoping that, if some poor soul should meet an unpleasant end in the ocean, you'd be among the first to hear about it. The English even had a prayer for the occasion:

> We pray thee, O Lord, not that wrecks should happen, but that if any shall happen, Thou wilt guide them onto our shores for the benefit of the inhabitants.

Wrecking, as it was called, has been popular on seacoasts around the world. On Cape Cod, wreckers were called mooncussers, for the simple reason that when the moon shone bright, ships were less likely to run aground. While there wasn't much to be done to darken the moon, there are countless stories of people shining lights from rowboats, or hanging lanterns from cows and walking them along the dark beach, to confuse helmsmen. If sailors were fortunate enough to survive a wreck, some mooncussers were willing to slit their throats. Wrecking was serious business.

Colonial authorities decreed that anyone who found any part of the cargo from a wreck had to report what he found to the town clerk, who would then be responsible for salvaging the wreck and holding the material for the vessel's owner. That law was obeyed about as often as the ones we have now against jaywalking. In 1854, when Henry David Thoreau stopped at Nauset Light, the keeper told him there was strong local objection to the building of a lighthouse for the logical reason that it was likely to reduce the number of shipwrecks.

A wreck didn't need to contain anything as exotic as gold or emeralds to warrant attention. Plenty of people had use for a ship's wood and rigging, and anyone with a boat could use a compass and signal flags; cargo was icing on the cake. When the steamer *Onandaga* ran aground in 1907, Cape Codders were delighted to help themselves to wrapping paper, shoes, and screen doors. As recently as 1974, Barnstable residents stripped the sloop *Trull* at Sandy Neck, and in 1982, when the *Venture I* became stranded outside Chatham Harbor, a group of modern-day wreckers removed her propeller and navigational equipment. Nevertheless, there aren't many mooncussers left. In something akin to the way privateering, or government-sanctioned looting of an enemy country's ships, was legal, but freelance piracy was not, the once-accepted tradition of wrecking is now regarded by most people as simple thievery.

From what I knew about the history of the cape, it seemed that everyone for miles around would have gone to the wreck site to get their hands on the treasure. As I read, though, I came to understand the primitive state of early wrecking. For the most part, people simply gathered whatever washed ashore or, in the case of an exposed wreck, waded or rowed to it and removed everything of value.

There would have been no wading to the *Whydah*—anyone foolish enough to be in the water would have died of hypothermia. And the pirate ship went down on the surf line, where the waves break—a treacherous area. Working on the surface there would have been—and still is—terribly difficult, even harder than working farther out to sea. The people didn't have diving equipment, of course, and even if the locals had waited for warmer weather, rowed to the site, held their breath, and dived—which I assumed some of them had—they would have only found whatever might have been lying in plain view.

The ocean floor off the cape is almost entirely sand. The surf keeps the sand constantly moving, so the topography of the floor changes hour to hour, sometimes dramatically. Even the sandbars shift. Add to that the strong currents—during a storm the strongest swimmer would have trouble making progress toward shore because everything is swept north (or south, depending upon the direction of the storm), parallel to the coast—and it seemed obvious that by the summer of 1717 virtually nothing from the ship would have been visible.

No, the more I read, the more I believed Bellamy's prize had escaped the schoolboys and farmers, sailors and smugglers who rushed to the scene.

. . .

When Thomas Davis told his story to Samuel Harding, the farmer hitched one of his horses to a wagon and headed to the shore to see if the *Whydah*'s cargo had washed up in the storm. It was daylight by the time they reached the shore, but still windy, cold, and raining. After heaping the wagon with the choicest of the items on the beach, they took the load back to the farm. Harding then shared the news with his brother, Abiah, and his neighbors Edward Knowles and Jonathan Cole.

While the entire population of the cape came to only a few thousand, with most of them on the inner, protected, side, over the next day or so two hundred men, women, and children braved the harsh weather to gather wreckage from the *Whydah*. The sea remained far too rough and cold to allow them to go out to the wreck, so those earliest salvagers had to content themselves with stacking onto carts and wagons enormous tangles of rope, large planks and fragments of wood, sails, ironware, and such buoyant goods as intact kegs of liquor and flour.

They didn't have much use for the corpses.

In the first few days fifty-four mutilated bodies washed up. Then twenty-two more. Eventually the coroner counted one hundred and one pirates crushed by cannon, skewered by splintering beams, strangled in twisted rigging, drowned under the hull, stripped naked by the force of the waves, and gnawed by crabs and lobsters. The bodies were so horrifyingly destroyed that some religious leaders conjectured—and the rumor became legend, as these things will— that the pirates had murdered each other. That probably seemed more reassuring to people who spent so much of their lives on water than the truth, which was that the ocean itself was responsible for such violence. But while some of the crowd may have drawn back respectfully, or in fright, other God-fearing Puritans quickly came forward to slice off the fingers and ears of Bellamy's crew in order to get at their rings and earrings.

After all, pirates were sinful, lawless men.

. . .

Like other rebels before and after them, pirates have been romanticized. Blackbeard is as compelling a legendary figure to people who grew up near the ocean as Jesse James is to Midwesterners. But the lives of sailors were at least as difficult and unenviable as the lives of early western settlers, and pirates, men escaping enslavement aboard ships, weren't laughing rogues with cursing parrots and countless bottles of rum. So while I found bits and pieces about Sam Bellamy in local libraries up and down the cape, I spent a lot of time separating information that was probably true from the merely plausible, the plausible from the absurd.

One of the earliest secondhand accounts of the wreck was written in 1724 by Daniel Defoe, in his *A General History of the Robberies and Murders of the Most Notorious Pirates,* originally published under the pseudonym Captain Charles Johnson. A wonderful writer, Defoe was passionate about the sea, and he interviewed a man held captive by Paulsgrave Williams not long after the wreck.

Relying on his discussions with the prisoner, Defoe describes in detail Bellamy's trip from Virginia to Block Island to Maine, where he had the crew stop to build a fort, back to the cape, and from there—

—but by then I had stopped taking notes, because the chronology was all wrong. Defoe had Bellamy making that trip, fort and all, in two weeks. He had also changed the times and places the pirates confronted merchant ships, directly contradicting what some of the sailors themselves had said. What sounded like a perfectly plausible narrative turned out to be worthless.

Defoe really puts his poetic license on the line when he tells a story about the crew's behavior after surviving a storm.

According to the author of *Robinson Crusoe,* Bellamy's men celebrated by performing *The Royal Pirate,* a play about Alexander the Great. When the pirate playing Alexander threatened to kill a pirate playing the role of a pirate, an overly passionate member of the audience rushed to the defense, lighting a grenade and throwing it at "Alexander." After the smoke cleared, the actor playing Alexander had lost an arm, another had broken a leg, and the serious fighting began. Bellamy ordered the unruliest men placed in chains for a day, then decreed that particular play would no longer be performed.

A novelist's imagination gone berserk, right?

Defoe may have exaggerated, but the story probably has some truth to it. Pirates, like all seamen, spent long months in confined spaces; forced to provide their own entertainment, they sang, played games (though pirate captains often forbade gambling), and acted out popular stories. So while it's not likely they were carrying scripts of the Greek tragedies, they might very well have performed for each other a play which did, after all, concern pirates. (And hand grenades, in case you're wondering, had already been around for over a hundred years. Bellamy's men favored an iron cannonball hollowed out and packed with gunpowder, lit with a fuse to a wooden plug.)

The only way to get at the reliable truth, I decided, was to study the few firsthand accounts of the wreck and its aftermath.

Ten miles south of the beach where Harding and Davis gathered all they could, Thomas Fitzgerald found his faith in prayer greatly strengthened.

Saturday's clouded dawn found the three sailors and seven pirates on the *Mary Anne* still alive. They were amazed to find they had survived their ship having been driven ashore on Pochet's Island, near Eastham. (Pochet's Island is opposite an inconsequential bit of swampland with a colorful history. In 1626 the *Sparrow Hawk* wrecked there, and among the passengers were a Mr. Fells and a woman he inconsistently referred to as his maid and housekeeper. The other passengers suspected the woman to be his mistress, and when they discovered she was pregnant they ostracized the young couple. So much for the unifying bond of shared hardship among America's pioneers. The two were abandoned by their fellow settlers at a spot known thereafter as Slut's Bush.)

Once on solid ground, Alexander Mackconachy, the *Mary Anne*'s fifty-five-year-old cook, established his priorities: with the help of two of the pirates, who brought out a chest of sweetmeats, he prepared a breakfast which, washed down with madeira, further raised the spirits of everyone at hand.

Thomas Fitzgerald soon noticed, though, that the pirates were gazing anxiously at the horizon, where there was no sign of their mates. Surviving the previous night's storm meant little if they were apprehended so near to Boston, a city known for dealing harshly with pirates.

Meanwhile, two men from Eastham, John Cole and William Smith, spotted the *Mary Anne* and decided to investigate. As they neared the ship in their canoe they found not an abandoned wreck, but ten bedraggled men, some in high spirits, some despondent. They seemed not so much a crew but ten strangers. Cole and Smith were willing to overlook their suspicions, though, when they learned the nature of the *Mary Anne*'s cargo. Offering to take the men to Eastham, they strongly suggested using demijohns and casks of Madeira to balance the canoe. As they assisted in procuring the necessary casks, they realized it might be best to make several trips.

When the twelve men reached John Cole's house overlooking the bay, it seemed only appropriate to celebrate. As they drank, the cook, Mackconachy, grew convinced he was in safe hands.

"These men," he said, indicating the seven from the *Whydah,* "are pirates every one, from the crew of Black Bellamy!"

"Our captain may be Bellamy," Baker quickly answered, "but we are no pirates. The captain is an Englishman with a commission from King George."

Simon Van Vorst laughed. "Ya, and we stretched it to the world's end!"

Cole doubted the story, but he knew the men had survived great hardship. Inviting them to stay and refresh themselves, he excused himself. In the back of the house he told his son to tell Mr. Doane, justice of the peace and representative to the Great and General Court, they had seven or possibly even ten pirates in the house.

Fully aware of the danger they faced, the pirates hastily thanked Cole, put on their hats, and ran. Searching for landmarks, they scrambled across the Burying Acre before sighting a tavern, where they hoped to find mounts. The justice and his posse caught the seven outside of the tavern, and Thomas South immediately began protesting.

"I never bore arms," he said as a deputy pulled his hands behind his back. "I was forced to join these men. I am an honest ship's carpenter, as God shall attest." He felt a thin rope cross over his wrists, and for a moment he must have believed they were all going to be hanged on the spot.

"You'll have your chance to plead," Justice Doane said.

Whatever hope South held out was diminished when he turned and saw the three honest sailors from the *Mary Anne,* including Fitzgerald and Mackconachy, being led toward the tavern by the deputy sheriff, their hands tied.

As they were marched down the King's Highway to Barnstable jail, the pirates began to confess.

Justice Doane listened carefully. That evening he reported to Colonel Buffet of Sandwich. The next morning, less than forty-eight hours after the wreck, the colonel sent a messenger to Samuel Shute, the new governor of the province of Massachusetts Bay, in Boston. The message, in part, read:

> The Pyrates . . . being examined by Justice Doane of Barnstable, the 27th of April past, whose Names are, Samuel Vanderson, Thomas Beaker, Thomas South, Peter Hove, John Sho, John Brown, Hendrick Quinter, all Foreigners, Mariners or Seamen, confessed that on the 26th past, between Nantucket Shoals and St. George's Banks, they had taken a ship called the Mary Anne, which was stranded on the Shore at Eastham, and that they belonged to a ship call'd Whido, Man'd with about 130 Men, 28 Guns, who had not any commission from any Prince or Potentate . . . on board whereof about 130 Men were drown'd and none saved except two . . . A great many Men have been taken up Dead near the Place where the Ship was cast away.

Like countless politicians before and since, Samuel Shute was immediately attracted to the idea of claiming easy money. British law of the time held that title to abandoned pirate property found on the sea was the prerogative of the Crown, and the governor had every reason to believe he would be personally rewarded for his efforts on behalf of the king. If the people of the cape had already salvaged most of what had washed ashore, so much the better—a representative of the government would merely need to go door-to-door and relieve the inhabitants of their illicitly gotten goods.

· · ·

Once I satisfied myself that the *Whydah* had carried at least as much treasure as Cape Codders claimed it had, I turned back to the man Shute chose as his representative, the one source my instincts told me was absolutely trustworthy: Captain Cyprian Southack.

Southack was, for a variety of reasons, the perfect man to investigate the scene of the wreck. The son of a British naval lieutenant, he had come to Boston at the age of twenty-three and immediately begun acquainting himself with both the land and the sea. In the thirty-two years since, he had enjoyed a long and successful career as a cartographer, creating, among others, a "Draught of New England, Newfoundland, Nova Scotia and the River of Canada" and "A Draught of Boston Harbor." He had commanded the *Province* galley in an expedition against the French and Indians in Maine and Nova Scotia and, more relevantly, commanded ships whose responsibility it was to protect the New England coast from privateers and pirates.

Nearly every written account of the *Whydah* mentions Southack; the historians relied on his notes, maps, and letters. But I wanted to read him for myself, both to see if there might be something the others had missed and to get a better sense of what it had felt like to be on the cape that April. As a veteran cartographer, Southack had trained himself to be precise; of all the people at the scene of the wreck, he was the only one who took detailed notes.

Most of Southack's original papers are included in the Massachusetts State Archives. I hunted them down, made copies of the relevant pages of his journal, and was totally absorbed by them. I nearly forgot I was in my house on present-day Martha's Vineyard. Loud giggling suddenly brought me back.

"Barry," Brigitta called from the other room.

"All right, all right."

I stood, stretched, and walked to the kids' rooms, working on a threatening voice. "Lights out, crew. I expect all of you up at sunrise."

Groans. Then Jenny said: "Tell us a story."

"No stories. You're already up way too late."

But then Brandon and Barry started in.

"Okay. One. But then in bed, lights out, and I don't want to hear so much as a cough out of you."

We sat in Jenny's room, Barry and Brandon settling down after a minute of pushing and bickering. Brandon sat at the foot of the bed, which I had built into the wall, like a ship's bed.

"This is a story," I began, "about the giant sea turtle."

"These are the best," Barry said.

The giant sea turtle starred in a long-running serial based on a simple premise: when we all rode on the turtle's back, we could breathe underwater. The turtle took us to wonderful places, places no one else had ever seen. Lately he had been taking us on tours of old wrecks.

When Barry and Jenny and Brandon were finally ready to sleep, I went back downstairs, spread the photocopies in the light of the lamp clipped to my desk, and went back to work.

Southack received his instructions Monday, and by Wednesday could write in his journal, "This morning at 10 Clock I came to Saile by order of his Excellency Samuel Shute Esq. in his Majesty's Hired Sloop Nathaniel." (An apology: Southack's punctuation and spelling can be distracting, I know. I've left them uncorrected to give you some small idea of what I was up against, and this isn't even the beginning: the man's handwriting is a researcher's nightmare. All loops and swirls, flourishes that were, at the time, the sign of an educated man. It's a nice effect from a distance, but if you're trying to read for content . . . you wouldn't bother unless you were a fanatic for history—or thought you'd find clues to buried treasure.)

On May 2 Southack and his men arrived at Cape Cod Harbor (now Provincetown Harbor; name changes are another problem with deciphering the journals). He immediately ordered two of his deputies, Cutler and Little, to take a whaleboat to Truro, where they acquired horses to carry them to the site of the wreck. Arriving that evening, they found a few people picking over what little was left to salvage. Sending them home, the two established a watch to discourage anyone similarly minded.

Southack wasn't dragging his feet; he knew that he was as likely to learn about the wreck in the harbor as he was at the site. On one ship he "found a Yung man boling [belonging] to the ship the Pirritt Took 26 April in South Channell, Saileing from Nantaskett the day before at 3 After noon." After interviewing that sailor and others, he set off in the predawn hours of the next morning for Truro, where he expected a horse to be awaiting him at the home of an aptly named Captain Pain. Not only was the horse not there, but there were no available horses in town.

It was an ominous beginning.

Anxious to reach the site before the locals could hide what they had salvaged, but forced to continue by whaleboat, the resourceful Southack remembered that an early English navigator had discovered a way to cross the cape to the ocean via tidal canals. Boatmeadow Creek led through meadows of salt hay from Barnstable Bay, while Jeremiah's Gutter led through marshland to Town Cove and eventually the Atlantic. The two passageways met only during high tides, but Southack was in luck: the morning of May 3 was the height of the spring tides.

That was the good news. The bad news was, thanks to the action of the cape's dynamic winds and waves during the hundred years since the passageway had been mapped, the canals had nearly disappeared (they're since long gone). Determined, the captain and his eight men attempted the crossing.

The oars of the whaleboat began scraping the banks almost immediately. Southack ordered two men to begin poling, or pushing off against the muck beneath. That worked for a while. When the boat became so firmly stuck on the mud that the oars threatened to snap, the men disembarked, leaving their "geer" aboard. Ever the optimist, Southack noted that as long as none of them rode in the boat, they could at least tie a line to the bow and pull it.

Not for long.

Though there was barely enough water to float their vessel, the men quickly discovered that the mud was wet and thick. Working against frigid winds and occasional drizzle, they slipped in the eelgrass, fell to their knees in slime, felt their boots sucked loose by the ooze. But if they thought that was bad, it was because they hadn't yet reached the marshland. There they made the long portage, lifting the boat on slender ash poles.

In Jeremiah's Gutter they reversed the process: towing, poling, then rowing. Once they reached Nauset Harbor, the men had to fight their way up the coast through the still-churning ocean. When Southack saw Cutler and Little on the beach, he ordered the men to halt—exhausted by the trip, they were happy to obey—so he could time the breakers. Capsizing would be the final irony in this trip plagued by low-water. Fortunately, the veteran commander guided the boat in safely.

The journey of fourteen hours to cover approximately twenty miles put the Captain in a sour mood; in his journal he recorded his disappointment that, instead of an intact ship stranded amid the waves, he found "the Pirate Wreck all to pieces North & South Distance from each other 4 miles." Worse, according to Justice Doane "there has been at least 200 men from Several places at 20 miles distance plundering the Pirate Wreck of what came ashoar."

The next day the captain pursued two courses of action. First, despite a strong gale and rain, he rowed with six men to what he sometimes refers to in his letters as "The Pirritt Rack." Due to the severity of the sea, he could do no more than locate "her Anchor where She Struck first." Back on shore, he ordered his men to collect what little the Cape Codders had left behind combined with whatever had washed ashore since Cutler and Little had arrived. Southack gave himself the task of counting the bodies, which at the time amounted to "54 white men and five negros out of the Pirate Wreck Dead." Then he placed an ad.

Whereas . . . His Excellency the Governor hath Authorized and impower'd me the Subscriber, to discover & take care of S. Wreck & to Impress men & whatsoever Else necessary to discover & Secure what may be part of her . . . with Orders to go into any house, Shop, Cellar, Warehouse, room or other place, & in case of resistance to break open any doors, Chests, trunks & other packages there to Seize & from thence to bring away any of the goods, Merchandize, Effects belonging to S. Wreck, as also to Seize any of her men.

He went on to say, with no trace of irony, that "all his Majesty's . . . loving Subjects are Hereby Commanded to be aiding and assisting to me . . . or they will answer if Contrary at their utmost peril." One gets the distinct impression that Captain Southack trusted the good people of Cape Cod about as much as they welcomed him.

Given the threat, the locals didn't exactly come running forward.

On May 6 Southack placed another ad, and for nearly a week he personally visited houses and shops, stooped through root cellars and attics, and rummaged through chests, trunks, and packages. He kicked at the straw in barns, felt for recently dug dirt under his boots, and leaned casually against fireplaces in search of the secret rooms settlers had built to hide from Indians.

Did the inhabitants resent his intrusion? Not to his face. Infuriatingly, they invited him to visit, to stay longer, to come again. Samuel Harding actually found the nerve to admit that he had cargo from the wreck, but felt he could not show it to the captain, much less turn it over, because he was holding the salvage for Thomas Davis, who was awaiting trial in Boston. As a man of honor, Harding went on, the captain must certainly see why his promise to the wrongfully charged stranger must be kept.

Southack wrote to the governor, "I find the said Harding is as Gilty as the Pirate Saved." Then he further elaborated the extent of his ordeal:

Sir . . . Gentt'men that I have Deputed, have Rid at Least Thirty miles a moung the Inhabtances, whome I have had Information of ther being at the Pirate Rack, and have Gott Concernable Riches out of her. . . . I shall Mention their Names to Your Excellency in Order for a Warrant to me for bringing them for boston before Your Excellency, or as You Pleass, Sir, for all thes Pepol are very stife [stiff] and will not one [own] Nothing of what they Gott.

Meanwhile, Southack climbed daily to what he called "Pirate Wreck Hill" overlooking the site, hoping to be able to take the whale boat out and begin "fishing" for what remained of the treasure by lowering buckets and dragging them over the wreck. But the weather, like the locals, refused to cooperate. "This morning the Wind at S a strong gale and rain," he had written on the fourth. "A great sea so that we can do nothing as yet." These conditions prevailed for four days. On the ninth he went out on the whaleboat, but the sea was still so disturbed that he "could see nothing for the sand making the water thick and muddey."

On his return to shore, he was presented with a coroner's bill of £83 for the burial of the dead pirates. Southack was working "out of pocket," expecting his expenses to be reimbursed by the governor. Even so, he refused to spend public money on criminals; he seems to have thought the coroner had intended to donate his services. The local man settled the dispute by putting a lien on what little salvage Southack had managed to collect. The captain fired off yet another letter to Governor Shute: "I am of the mind that the Curner . . . should have nothing for buering aney of thes men . . . I humbley Desier Your Excellency Orders to this Afare. the Curner name is Samuell freeman for his stoping any of the Rack Goods for Paye is very hard." As for the wreck itself, he could only report that he could "se the Anchor Every Loaw Watter."

Turning his attention to the *Mary Anne* ten miles distant, Southack's luck wasn't much better. His men were able to gather some line and other supplies, but every last demijohn of Madeira had been appropriated by fast-working locals. Southack did discover, however, some useful information. He warned the governor that "the Pirate Sloop and snow Tender to the Ship Lost area bound to Cape Sables to Clean . . . our Ships from England will be in Great Danger of failing into Their hands, If some Care be not Taken."

Sitting at my desk for hours isn't the sort of work I usually enjoy, but reading Southack I felt like Sherlock Holmes when the game is afoot. I grew convinced Southack had been meticulous, despite his frustrations. But while I kept staring at his maps, no watery X ever rose to the surface. Some nights after I went to bed, bleary-eyed, I'd be drifting into sleep when suddenly Southack seemed to speak to me—I'd run into the next room, switch on the desk lamp, and try to hear what he was saying.

It wasn't enough to know that the *Whydah* lay somewhere near Wellfleet. If the ocean floor were coral, or rock, and the water were clear, it might have been possible simply to start diving, looking for signs of the ship, the way a helicopter might fly over a jungle to look for a wrecked plane. But the *Whydah*'s treasure was buried in sand, and getting under 250 years of it was going to be slow, expensive work.

I soon found out I could only have the opportunity to do that work after a state regulatory group called the Massachusetts Board of Underwater Archaeological Resources granted me a permit, and they would only grant a permit for a very specific request area backed by strong supporting evidence. Even then, I knew they'd give me a fight.

I had first crossed paths with the board in 1976 when, at the suggestion of the curator of the Pilgrim Museum in Plymouth, I began searching for the *General Arnold*, a revolutionary warship. Late in December the *Arnold* had come into Plymouth Harbor to escape a storm only to be driven into a sandbar. Most of the passengers froze to death and were buried in a mass grave, some of them still frozen together.

After completing an aerial survey, I hired an eastern-rigged dragger called the *Mars* to take me into the harbor. The water was shallow; I poked around, found the ribs of a ship, and applied for a permit from the board. A few days later I got a call from a somewhat puzzled board member who told me the captain of the *Mars* had filed an identical application.

Until that time, the Board of Underwater Archaeological Resources had not been what you would call overworked. At their meetings they wore shorts and T-shirts or whatever they happened to be wearing, occasionally issuing a permit, but generally talking among themselves. To make matters worse, when they met to discuss the disputed permit territory, a local surveyor named Charles Sanderson claimed his family had been diving the wreck for years, so the privilege of unearthing the wreck for the museum rightfully belonged to him.

The long story short: everyone sued everyone, the Pilgrim Society was mortified (that's the way those people talk: "We're mortified," they'd say, "Absolutely mortified,"), my lawyer, Allan Tufankjian, reviewed the Admiralty issues and handled the case for me, I won a permit—

—and, after doing some more research, realized the ship I had found wasn't the *General Arnold* after all. In fact, there was good evidence that the *Arnold* had been refloated the spring after it wrecked.

To say that incident left bad blood between me and the board is like saying dogs aren't crazy about cats. So while Southack had actually written on his map the caption "The Pirate Ship Whido Lost," the space covered by those words corresponded to about ten square miles of ocean—and I knew the board was going to need solid evidence.

Sitting at my drafting table, thumbing through the pages of Southack's journal, it stopped making sense. You know how, when you read something too many times, you can't really read it any more? I tried to concentrate, but all I saw was what I had already seen and noted in the margins. Then I came across something so obvious that I had looked right past it a hundred times.

On May 4 Southack wrote that he was collecting pieces of cable washed ashore from the *Whydah* and transporting them by land to a vessel moored in a bayside town. Taking the cable to a vessel on the seaboard side would have been too dangerous, Southack explained, because there was "no Harbour in 25 miles of the wreck." Every other time I had read that sentence I had assumed Southack was merely saying there was no harbor nearby. This time I realized that he wouldn't have specified twenty-five miles for no reason; it was a backward way of saying the nearest harbor, which would have been Cape Cod Harbor, was twenty-five miles away.

Of course, twenty-five miles was something of an approximation. But in the very same sentence he said it was "but 3½ miles from the wreck to Billingsgate," the bayside town where they were collecting the cable.

I didn't even waste time telling myself how stupid I had been to miss these clues for so long. I just placed the point of my compass on the map, drew an arc that represented everything on the ocean side of the cape twenty-five miles from Provincetown, the town at the harbor, then went to set the point of the compass on Billingsgate—

—which doesn't exist.

I was standing at the door of the public library when it opened. I hadn't slept, hadn't showered, hadn't eaten, nothing. I searched through some local histories for a reference to Billingsgate, Billingsgate . . . and found it. I knew of Billingsgate *Shoal*, but that morning I learned that Billingsgate had been a town near present-day Wellfleet. Terrific, I thought. Wonderful. Right here under my nose. I started laughing, which was a mistake; Cape Cod librarians don't appreciate large unwashed men chortling in the stacks. Lucky for them, I kept reading.

Billingsgate had been under water for about a hundred years.

It took a few days to learn that only part of the town was submerged; the rest was still part of Wellfleet. Once I knew that, though, I still had to decide where to measure from. Trusting in Southack, I assumed he gave his distance from the center of town. The town center in any New England community in those days was the church, so I set out on foot, combing through cemeteries, reading dates from worn, moss-covered tombstones. By the end of the week, I knew where to set the point of my compass.

When I wasn't poring over photocopied manuscripts on the Vineyard, I spent as much time as I could on the cape, talking to local historians, amateur historians, old salts who eventually came around to the topic if you waited long enough, and bartenders, who hear any gossip worth hearing. I searched through the small, quaint town libraries and found less than I had hoped. Writer after writer claimed that the mooncussers probably found most of the treasure, and I was convinced they couldn't have dived the wreck, especially considering the weather and the season. That's when I decided it was a mistake to rely too much on new books and articles. I was back where I'd started: if anyone could be trusted to have useful information, it was the people who had been closest to the wreck around the time that it happened, before all the stories were embroidered, before the history grew clouded by legend.

Each of the captured pirates had been questioned from the moment they were caught until the nooses were looped around their necks, and all of their testimony still exists in court records. John Brown said, "It was the common report . . . that they had about 20,000 pounds in gold and silver." Thomas Baker said the number may have been as high as 30,000, and added "the Quartermaster declared to the company, that if any man wanted money he might have it." Peter Hoof agreed with the higher estimate and said the coins and other riches were "counted over in the cabin, and put up in bags, fifty pounds to every man's share, there being 180 men on board. Their money was kept in chests between decks without any guard." Fifty pounds each for 180 men works out to about 9,000 pounds, which meant there had been four and a half tons of treasure worth £20,000–£30,000 sterling—and that appeared to include only the treasure captured on the *Whydah*. Unlike some of the people I talked to, I don't think the pirates would have exaggerated their success; on the contrary, they would have tried to convince the court they hadn't robbed or endangered anyone.

All this meant there must be plenty left for me.

The pirates on the *Anne* and the *Fisher* fared far better. Dropping anchor not far from the *Whydah*, they managed to ride out the storm. The following morning the *Fisher* was looted, its prize crew, captives, and cargo brought aboard the *Anne*. The *Fisher*'s hatches were opened and the vessel abandoned at sea as the *Anne* made for Menhagen, Maine, to rendezvous with the *Whydah*, which they assumed had survived.

When Bellamy failed to arrive, the pirates aboard the *Anne*, commanded by Noland, picked up where they left off, busily looting ships along the coast on their way to the Bahamas. A year later Noland accepted King George I's pardon and turned more or less respectable.

Paulsgrave Williams had spent the night of the storm on Block Island, visiting his mother and sisters. Two days later he and his men in the sloop *Mary Ann* (not to be confused with the *Anne* or the *Mary Anne*—ship owners weren't so creative with names back then) reached the site of the wreck. Williams ordered a boat to survey the site, but they had no luck. After pursuing a few of the local fishing vessels, Williams continued northward to the rendezvous site.

By the time they reached Spurwinke, Maine, the crew had been supplemented by pirates and prisoners aboard an accompanying sloop and shallop. The pirates proceeded to the nearest house, the residence of a Mr. Geordan. At the sight of his approaching guests, Mr. Geordan is reported to have fled into the woods.

At Damaries Cove, Williams had the *Mary Ann* careened, or laid over for maintenance. When that was finished, the men returned south, capturing another vessel at Cape Elizabeth before reaching Cape Cod three weeks after the wreck. There Williams spoke with several local men and learned what he had feared: nearly all of the *Whydah*'s crew had died, the few survivors imprisoned. He gave the sailors a warning: if the pirates in the Boston jail suffered, he and his men would kill every sailor they captured belonging to New England.

Southack had known what he was talking about when he warned his governor of the potential danger of nearby pirates. Williams and his men remained active, and on May 21 the Massachusetts lieutenant governor dispatched two ships and over one hundred well-armed men to discourage them. In the first week they spotted Williams twice. On May 30 a Captain Coffin interviewed a number of men who admitted having spoken with the pirate captain.

That's as close as he got.

Content with being New England's most wanted man for the better part of a month, Williams eluded the five ships whose sole purpose was to stop him. The following year he also took the king's pardon, but soon decided he preferred freedom to respectability. After going on to hijack ships with several more crews, Williams finally "retired" in 1723. He died peacefully in Rhode Island.

Thomas Davis became gravely ill as a result of his exposure during the storm and his exertions with Harding. After being given medical treatment, he found himself imprisoned with the others.

By that time Thomas South had heard the details of the wreck. He could not have been more surprised to find his friend alive. Still, neither of them could find much cause for celebration in their reunion. The governor let all of the accused contemplate their dark future at excruciating length. The group remained chained in close quarters in the hot, foul prison through the entire summer and into the fall.

South had never been as vocal about his desire to leave the *Whydah,* so had been accepted by the crew. Now, though, he worried that the stern court would see no reason to differentiate him from the others. They would certainly all look alike to the representatives of justice: young, strong, and dirty. And by sentencing them severely, the court might feel it had taken some small revenge for the theft and murder that had plagued the province's merchants and traders.

Davis, who shared South's concern, explained his own predicament to the prison-keeper and begged to be held in a separate cell to await trial.

During those five months, the men had one frequent visitor: Cotton Mather. A member of Puritan New England's most famous family of clergy and statesmen, Mather relished his role as a Christian leader. As a child he wrote prayers and distributed them among his young schoolmates, who responded by pummeling him. Undeterred, he entered Harvard at age twelve, preached his first sermon at age sixteen, and set about achieving any number of admirable goals: improving the living conditions of widows and orphans, distributing food and providing education for the needy, and maintaining a school for Negroes.

While he may have had good intentions, Mather's social skills weren't the strongest. Even in the context of the Puritan community of the early eighteenth century, he was a fanatic. Once the minister threatened to leave Boston, where he felt he had been opposed at every turn, people reacted in two ways. Some taunted him, saying he was admitting defeat to the devil. The others offered to help him pack.

Furious, Mather stayed. And when he learned that a captive audience awaited him in the Boston jail, he saw the challenge of a lifetime. Understand, Mather saw *himself* as an indescribably filthy sinner in the eyes of God. If he could save these poor souls, perhaps he could convince himself, if not of his own worth, then of the value of his life's mission.

So in addition to cramped confinement, terrible heat, tremendous anxiety, and bad food (gone were the days of Madeira, rum, and a menu that varied with each captured ship's stores), the prisoners were now subjected to countless sermons and remonstrances by Cotton Mather. Preaching, like justice, was a long-winded affair in those days, so the better part of a morning or afternoon might be taken up by one of Mather's sermons. Mather terrorized them, he pleaded with them, he wrote each man a confession and rehearsed them like a choir.

Like the sinners of his dreams, they asked for more.

Baker, Brown, and the others were no fools. They knew that if one man could save them, could convince the court that they had atoned for the sins of their youth and pledged to reform, it was this over-weight, sanctimonious, wig-wearing preacher.

What they didn't understand was that Cotton Mather had only passing interest in this earthly world; he intended not to save their lives, but to prepare their souls for God.

A Judiciary Court of Admiralty assembled in the Boston courthouse on Friday, October 18, 1717. Twelve judges were gathered, including Governor Shute and Lieutenant Governor William Dummer.

His Majesty's advocate, a Mr. Smith, defined piracy as "treason, oppression, murder, assassination, robbery and theft . . . committed where the weak and defenseless can expect no assistance or relief." If Sam Bellamy had been in the courtroom, he would have been furious. Those, he would have told Smith, were exactly the practices of merchants and sea captains that pirates fought to escape.

Thomas South, looking the judges in the eye, argued that he had been forced to join the others, and that his only chances for escape had come on desolate islands, where he believed it unlikely he could survive.

Each of the pirates proceeded to make exactly the same argument.

Mr. Smith responded by saying that "their pretence of being forced out of their respective ships . . . can never excuse their guilt, since no case of necessity can justify a direct violation of the Divine and Moral Law." After reviewing the evidence, the judges found Van Vorst, Brown, Baker, Quintor, Hoof, and Shuan guilty of piracy, robbery, and felony.

South was found not guilty. Three witnesses who had been held in prison were paid for their trouble and dismissed.

Thomas Davis's trial began on Monday, October 28th. The

twenty-two-year-old carpenter was charged, and Mr. Smith asked that he be punished by death "to the example and terror of others to do or commit the like crimes in times coming."

To their credit, the judges spent little time deciding the defendent had been forced to stay on the *Whydah* against his will.

Cotton Mather's work, of course, was not finished. He accompanied the convicted men from the jail on the wintry afternoon of November 15. Dozens of men surrounded the pirates lest they try to escape; but it was far too late for that. Surrounded by a mob of spectators, they proceeded through Boston and then by rowboat to a strip of shore between the high- and low-water marks of Charlestown.

Despite all his efforts, Mather had not quite made his position clear to the doomed men; they believed they might still stand some chance of being reprieved. So when the minister asked, "How do you find your heart now disposed?" they answered as he had trained them.

"Oh! I am in a dreadful Condition!" Baker shouted. "Lord JESUS, Dear JESUS, Look upon me!"

"You have been a very great sinner," Mather prodded.

"Oh! Yes; I am!" Baker agreed.

Moving on to Van Vorst, Mather asked which sins the man most regretted.

Van Vorst answered, "My undutifulness unto my parents and my profanation of the Sabbath."

"Say now," Mather asked, "what think you of the Bad Life, wherein you have Wandered from God? Can you say nothing that your Worthy Parents may take a little comfort from?"

Van Vorst answered, "I am heartily sorry for my very bad life."

The scripted confessions went on at length. Some of the men continued to claim that they had been forced; others repented for their misdeeds, though none quite as sincerely and loudly as Mather hoped. Meanwhile, the spectators had other concerns.

"Where's the gold?" they shouted. "Where are the jewels?"

Ignoring them, Mather asked Brown if he had any special sins he might like to mention.

"Special Sins!" Brown shouted, suddenly remembering his hours of rehearsal in jail. "Why, I have been guilty of all the Sins in the World! I know not where to begin. I may begin with Gaming!"

Mather cleared his throat.

Brown thought for a moment. "No, Whoring! That led on to Gaming; and Gaming Led on to Drinking; and Drinking to Lying, and Swearing and Cursing, and all that is bad; and so to Thieving; And so to this!"

The harbor's normal activity became paralyzed by the movement of the crowd, who vied for the best viewing positions as the six pirates were escorted to the scaffold. Mather continued droning even as the hempen loops were placed around their necks and pulled snug.

Though the pirates couldn't follow the example of the schoolboys who had pummeled the minister for his trouble, they could still speak for themselves. Unwilling to continue the hypocrisy of having fought for his freedom only to die apologizing for a life of drinking and swearing, John Brown suddenly took up swearing again, with renewed vigor. He cursed the crowd, cursed the country about to kill him. While he advised sailors to avoid taking up with pirates, he advised them even more strongly that if they did become pirates, they should take care what prisoners they released, and where they went ashore. When he paused for breath, the scaffold was released.

The six young men jumped and twitched. In accordance with the law, their bodies were left hanging through sunset, into the night, and into the dark of early morning, left swinging gently "within flux and reflux of the sea."

In his diary, the disappointed Mather wrote, "With such Madness, Go the Dead."

Cyprian Southack suffered three final indignities as a result of his mission on the coast.

After spending more than a week in miserable, wet weather, traveling by horseback and whaleboat, he contracted a chest cold. Then, in June, the materials he had salvaged from the *Whydah* were displayed at the Treasurer's Warehouse, to be auctioned off at the end of July. The items brought in £265, just barely enough to cover

Southack's expenses. A man present at the auction noted that the offerings included "two anchors, two great guns, and some junk."

The final insult took shape in the months and years after Southack returned to Boston. Some Cape Codders speculated that the captain had found much more than he let on. Certainly none of *them* had anything like the riches rumored to have been on the ship, and they had seen the outsider's whaleboat hovering over the wreck. In Crosby's and Higgins' taverns, in front of fireplaces in homes and farmhouses, they said Southack had only pretended to be frustrated, in order to support his letters to the governor. While he claimed not to have found anything of value, in fact he had smuggled coins and jewels beneath piles of worn and splintered planks. By the end of the winter people who had at first been grateful for free supplies of rope and wood envied the wily captain who had duped them and now, according to the latest version of the story, had taken a Creole mistress and returned to England.

The truth was less scandalous.

Southack recovered from his frustration on the cape. He published the "New England Coasting Pilot" in 1720 and a variety of other maps and charts renowned for their accuracy, documents that continued to be of great use to mariners long after his death. As far as his absconding with illicit riches is concerned, he wrote in his last letter to Governor Shute from the cape, dated May 13, "I am afears that when weather Permitts to goe off, the Riches with the guns would be Buried in the Sand." Cyprian Southack was far from the last man to be frustrated in his attempts to raise the treasure of the *Whydah*.

In *Cape Cod*, Thoreau repeats a bit of local lore:

> For many years after this shipwreck, a man of a very singular and frightful aspect used every spring and autumn to be seen travelling on the Cape, who was supposed to have been one of Bellamy's crew. The presumption is that he went to some place where money had been secreted by the pirates, to get such a supply as his exigencies required. When he died, many pieces of gold were found in a girdle which he constantly wore.

By the time I read that, I recognized it as the Southack rumor, with a twist. Other versions claim that John Julian (who most likely died awaiting trial) or Maria Hallett had access to the treasure.

Maria Hallett is a Cape Cod legend. One of the variations of her story has her living off a secret source of income, assumed to be part of the Whydah's treasure, which was somehow delivered to her; another claims that, denied her share of Bellamy's gold, Maria spent her adult life cursing every ship that passed the Cape's elbow. She was able to send ships and sailors to their doom, the old-timers say, because she was a witch.

Seven months after Bellamy set off to find his fortune, Maria gave birth to a black-haired boy. One of the reasons she moved to her own hut was to keep her condition a secret—Puritans were notoriously unsympathetic to unwed mothers. When the baby was born, Maria hid him in the Knowles barn, where he choked to death on a piece of straw. Elder John Knowles discovered the body, hid in the hay, and caught Maria when she came to feed her infant.

For her "crimes" of pregnancy and neglect, she was imprisoned in Eastham. Her jailors, either unusually liberal-minded or charmed, allowed her to escape. The sheriff ordered her brought back, but again the jailors left her cell unlocked. They couldn't admit it, of course, so the locals gave her the title that seemed to fit best. Though she was never tried, people believed her to be a witch, and Maria went on to live the rest of her life in isolation—with no treasure, I always believed, other than the memory of that summer with Sam Bellamy.

The ultimate variation of the hidden treasure story, recorded late in the nineteenth century, must have first been told much earlier:

A tall stranger appeared at Higgins' Tavern in the autumn of 1717. The stranger had long black hair and a deep white wound across his forehead. Though he took no job, he never seemed in need of money. Often he wandered through the Burying Acre to an apple tree, where he sat as if waiting for someone. In the summer of 1720, that's where his body was discovered.

While I'd like to believe the captain had the courage and strength and cleverness to survive, the seaman in me has convinced the romantic that Bellamy probably died on his flagship along with his men, egalitarian to the end. The real question is, did his body wash ashore with the others? Or were his bones anchored under the sand by his final prize?

One last research project remained for me on dry land and that was to determine the extent of any serious attempts at salvaging the *Whydah*. Late in the eighteenth century, Reverend Levi Whitman discussed the *Whydah* in "A Topographical Description of Wellfleet in the County of Barnstable." Whitman said coins from the wreck still washed ashore, and at times the iron caboose of the ship was visible above the surface. From what I know now, it seems unlikely that ship was the *Whydah*, but people were still desperately searching. Over fifty years later, Thoreau quoted the minister, adding that he himself chanced upon a French crown piece. The coin was "of a dark slate color, and looked like a flat pebble . . . I thought at first that it was that same old button which I have found so many times." Thoreau's coin, though, was dated 1741, and could have come from any one of hundreds of wrecks.

The one major effort to find the treasure earlier in this century was made by Edward Rowe Snow, the author. I read his books as a boy, and he seemed to know more about wrecks than anyone. In 1947 he spent a lot of money building a fifteen-foot diving platform over what he thought was the site, nearly lost a man from drowning, then saw a storm destroy the platform.

Uncle Bill's friend, Jack Poole, had been one of Snow's divers, and Poole convinced Bill they had found the wreck. They actually claimed to have found some silver coins and cannonballs—but again, these could have come from a number of ships. Estimating the value of what they found at about one-fortieth of what he had spent, Snow decided it wasn't worth the expense and the risk to salvor's lives to continue his efforts.

Thanks to what I heard from Bill, I never believed anyone had secretly gotten the treasure off the wreck. Too much work was involved; the story would have leaked out; and more than that, the necessary equipment simply hadn't existed. Diving wasn't enough; to get the majority of any wreck off the cape, you need to dig into the sand, all the way to the clay ten to twenty feet down.

Still, there were lessons to be learned from all of the earlier efforts.

By this time I had turned one room of our house on the Vineyard into a map room; I typed out a line of Edward Snow's and tacked it to the wall directly above my desk:

It will be a very lucky treasure hunter who ever does more than pay expenses while attempting to find the elusive gold and silver still aboard the Whydah.

To either side, and on the other walls, I posted copies of Southack's maps, aerial photographs of the coast, and other historical and contemporary maps reflecting the changing shoreline, all studded with red and blue and green and yellow push pins. Surrounded with information, I knew I still didn't have the key . . . I couldn't convince myself, much less anyone else, that I could go out onto the water and identify the exact spot where the *Whydah* lay.

As I talked to local people, I sometimes thought, *Southack must have walked this street; he must have stopped at this tavern.* The cape isn't that large; Southack and I covered the same ground, interviewing people, searching for virtually the same information. He became my touchstone. Early in the morning, before I was fully awake, I'd try to will dreams, imagining myself as the captain and cartographer. The one thing he knew that I didn't was the exact location of the wreck; he just lacked the equipment to reach it. I could get the equipment, but . . .

Sitting in the map room, I read his journal again and again. I took heart in the fact that while most of the historians quoted Southack as saying two hundred men from twenty miles distant had plundered the wreck, he actually said those locals plundered *what came ashore.* The wreck remained untouched.

One early morning when the sunlight barely filtered in through thick fog, I forced myself to look over my initial notes, more out of frustration than belief that I'd discover anything new—and that's how I found Southack's final clue.

In a letter written on May 8, he briefly told Governor Shute what Samuel Harding had said: that Thomas Davis had managed to find his house in the early hours of the morning after the storm.

After a smalle time, the said harding took the English man on his
Horse and carried him to the Rack. thes Two made Severall Turnes
from the Rack to harding's house, so they must Gott much riches.

Harding's house, Southack noted, was "two miles from the Rack."
I had made a note in the margin next to that entry the first time
I read it, but hadn't pursued it. The odds of finding Harding's home
seemed slim. If most of a town had been submerged, there was no
telling what had happened to a single farmhouse; it's not as if there
would be an historic plaque mounted next to the front door. Even
on the cape, where people have a strong sense of family history, I
doubted I'd stumble across someone who could tell me the story of
an unremarkable farmer. The only way to discover the location of
the house would be to find someone who knew about land transac-
tions, who had access to old deeds.

I learned early on in the salvaging business that it's a mistake to
tell people too much about what you're doing; in fact, sometimes it's
necessary to mislead them. So when I called Slade Associates, a
surveyor in Wellfleet, I simply told them I had an interest in local
history, which was true enough.

"Whose house?" the surveyor asked again, starting to take notes.

"Samuel Harding," I said. "This was around 1717." I told him
my one clue with regard to its location.

"When did he build the house, or take possession?"

I had no idea.

"Do you know when he might have sold it?"

"I don't know anything," I told him. "His name was Samuel
Harding, he had a farmhouse, his brother lived nearby."

"But he did own the farm."

I doodled on the back of an old letter on my desk.

"Mr. Clifford?"

"I don't know," I told him. "I hope so."

First I had jotted down the surveyor's fee; now, next to it, I wrote
Dead End.

TREASURE FEVER

AFTER GETTING OFF THE PHONE with the surveyor, I walked outside, where Birgitta was turning the vegetable garden.

"Damned ocean."

Birgitta looked out toward the water. "What's wrong with it?"

"It's huge."

Did she sympathize? Did she say I had a good point?

No. What she said was, "This is news?"

I no longer expected her to understand. I must have said that aloud, because she said "Understand what?" but by then I was already on my way back inside.

My obsession with the *Whydah* was driving Birgitta nuts. I admit, I had become something of a bore on the subject; I could see that, but it wasn't going to stop me.

I was too close to give up. If I couldn't pinpoint the wreck, I could get credibility another way, and maybe get some help at the same time.

Since late summer I had been trying to convince Mel Fisher to fly up from Key West and go out to the site. I never told him how vaguely defined "the site" was.

Fisher grew up in Indiana, about as far inland as you can get. After serving in World War II, he moved to Tampa, where he spent time in the water. Scuba gear—regulators, dive tanks, and wet suits—had been perfected by Jacques Cousteau for navy frogmen, so diving was virtually a new sport, something like bungee jumping today. Mel saw undersea treasure for the first time off St. Petersburg and started diving on wrecks. Soon he moved again, this time to California, where he and his father built a chicken ranch, but Mel had come down with a bad case of treasure fever. He invented a small gold dredge and started leading teams into the mountains to look for gold in streams.

That didn't pan out, but after trying a few other schemes, Fisher met up with Kip Wagner, a Florida treasure hunter who knew he was onto something big. Beginning in 1963, the two worked together, and over the next two years they couldn't miss. They found thousands of gold and silver coins, rare porcelain, and countless other artifacts. *National Geographic* did an article on their discoveries in 1965, but Mel went on to even bigger things. In 1973 he discovered the *Nuestra Señora de Atocha*, which had sunk in 1622, and a few years later her sister ship, the galleon *Santa margarita*, which contained a fabulous amount of gold.

Now, though, Mel was in trouble. Sued by the state of Florida and by other treasure hunters, he was about to go to trial there. After having lost his son, his daughter-in-law, and another diver when a salvage tug sank, he had become ill. On top of those personal problems, he was haunted by the fact that while he had found the *Atocha*, he hadn't been able to locate most of her treasure. (At one point Mel offered me half the value of the *Atocha* for half the value of the *Whydah* on a paper napkin. I turned him down. What neither of us knew in 1982, of course, was that three years later he would find the mother lode of the *Atocha*, millions of dollars worth of gold, silver, and jewels.) When I had talked to him, he sounded interested in the *Whydah*.

Mel had learned a lot about how to use the press. His work had been the subject of articles in all the major papers, the treasure he had found had been featured in an enormous exhibit in Washington, D.C., and on television specials. Mel told me that if word got out he believed I had found the *Whydah*, the media would pick up on it, and I'd have a much easier time raising money.

More than that, there were some things I needed to know about the equipment he had developed with the help of Fay Feild, his right-hand man. Besides, Mel had a strange, appropriate connection to the *Whydah*. He and his divers had once found part of what Bellamy had set off after: the Silver Plate Fleet that went down in 1715.

I let the phone ring off the hook.

"Mel," I said when he finally answered. "Barry Clifford. How's everything?"

"Do you have a lawyer?"

That's what he said. Not hello, how are things going, nothing: "Do you have a lawyer?"

"Sure," I said. "Why?"

"Pay him on time," Mel said. "You're going to need him as long as you're in this business."

I wrote that off as the advice of a man who had made some mistakes. I asked when he and Fay could come up.

"This is a bad time," Mel said. "I've got to be here until we're through with this thing in Miami, and we're having some trouble with one of the boats. I'll give you a call, all right?"

I hung up. Then I spent the better part of an hour staring out at that damned ocean.

A week or so later I was wrestling with Barry Jr. before dinner when Birgitta said, "I forgot to tell you—you got a call this afternoon. I left the note on your desk."

Breathing heavily—already, as an eleven-year-old, Barry was strong and fast—I went into the map room and saw a vaguely familiar phone number on my pad. It was after five, so I almost didn't bother, but then decided to try anyway.

It was Slade Associates. The woman on the phone told me the surveyor hadn't left yet, and when I heard him pick up the line I didn't even let him say hello.

"What did you get?"

Silence.

Then: "May I ask who's calling?"

"Barry Clifford, returning your call, you called earlier, what have you got?"

"This was . . . the Harding house."

"Right." I switched the phone to the other ear. This guy was taking forever.

"It stood about one mile from Whitecrest Beach, or one quarter mile southwest of Duck Pond."

"You found Harding's house?"

"Well, no. The house itself no longer stands, but I've gathered what we learned about the property, with mention of a few land-marks that may or may not be useful to you."

He sounded disappointed, but I didn't need to be able to stand on Harding's front porch; as I hung up I was adjusting my compass.

All of Southack's distances were rounded to the nearest half mile. The coastline had moved at least a thousand feet inland since South-ack made his notes, and 265 years of breaking surf must have had some effect on whatever remained, no matter how heavy. Even so, using Billingsgate, Provincetown, and now Harding's house, I could triangulate the *Whydah*'s position when she went down.

So while the margin of error was still too big, at least I had an X marking the theoretical spot, one that was supported by reliable evidence. The good and bad news was that, according to Peter Hoof, the treasure had been kept "in chests between decks," and Thomas Davis said "the riches on board were laid together in one heap." The *Whydah*'s wealth had fallen into the sea exactly as it had been stored: in one pile. That meant I was searching for a single needle in a buried, underwater haystack—but it also meant, when I found it, I would find it all.

Without a doubt, the question I've most often been asked in the last ten years is whether my primary interest in the *Whydah* lay in making money. Most people who ask that think they already know the answer, so it's a waste of breath trying to explain; what I tell them depends on my mood. The truth is this:

I live an unusual life—I don't go to an office, I don't have a boss, I only hire people temporarily. Believe me, it doesn't speed things up any when, on the "occupation" space on a credit card application, you write "treasure hunter." In order to continue doing what I love to do, I need to make a profit—just like any blue suit on Wall Street. To that extent, I have to keep an eye on the bottom line.

At the same time, I didn't have to talk to Edward Rowe Snow to realize that the *Whydah* was a long shot. Going after Bellamy's ship was going to cost a lot of money, and while Southack had put me on the right trail, everything I knew about treasure hunting convinced me that, 99 percent of the time, it's a losing proposition. My salvage work on the *Islander* didn't involve a search, just a fair fee for a difficult job, and even then I had to risk my life, wait eight years, and spend more than you'd believe in lawyer's fees before I got paid.

There are a lot of ways to die underwater. The more time you spend on a boat, especially in the sort of waters that destroyed the *Whydah,* the better the odds are that you'll run into serious trouble. To take that kind of chance, you have to really want something. What I wanted was Bellamy's ship—the cannon his men had fired, the stove that cooked his food, the pistol he wore. I wanted to prove Uncle Bill and Southack had been right, to prove generations of gossips had been wrong, and not least of all to bring Sam Bellamy to life. Pirates were part of an abused and repressed underclass; they faced a life with no opportunity for anything but lateral movement in their society, and they fought against that the best way they could. Bellamy had a story to tell, and I wanted the chance to tell it.

So, long before I started, I knew there were plenty of easier ways to make money. What I hadn't counted on were the bureacratic obstacles.

The Board of Underwater Archaeological Resources was a perfect example of Catch-22: I couldn't gather artifacts from the site until I had a permit, but I couldn't have a permit until I presented them with artifacts from the site. Who needs this? I thought. What kind of craziness is going on here? It was maddening to think that all the years of planning, all the years of reading and studying, would be wasted because of some absurd regulation.

But satisfying the board on that point turned out to be ridiculously simple. I got a man with a metal detector to search the beach along the area I'd marked on my map, hoping he might come across flotsam. In just a matter of weeks he turned up a few nails, coins, and some glass that might well have dated from the *Whydah* era—though they might not have. But combined with my research, my notes from Southack, and a compendium of tales I'd gathered from local people who had found genuine pre-1715 coins on that same stretch of beach, those objects convinced the board that I was on to something. There was a shipwreck out there, they agreed, though which ship it was, and precisely where it was located, remained to be seen.

. . .

"What are you doing?"

Birgitta stood in the doorway to my chart room, ready for bed. The kids were already asleep.

"Just going over a few things."

"What's to go over? There's nothing on those maps that wasn't there before dinner, or last night, or the night before."

Just to set the record straight, I wasn't looking at the maps—I was re-reading the pirates' testimony, trying to see if they mentioned anything specific from the ship that we might find to prove it was the *Whydah*.

All I said was, "I'll be there in a little while."

She sighed one of those dangerous sighs, and then she was gone.

So when the phone rang I picked it up fast, to keep it from waking any of them.

"Barry? Mel."

"Hi, Mel. Congratulations." I had followed the court case in Miami; he had been awarded rights to the *Margarita*.

"How do I find your place?"

"My house?"

"Wait a minute . . . she put the papers . . ." The phone hit a desktop with a clunk, then silence.

He came back. "The ticket says 8:58. So nine o'clock. That's when we get in."

"Nine o'clock when?"

"Tomorrow morning. We'll have the mag. You've got the boat, right?"

"Absolutely," I said. "Let's get to work."

As soon as I could get Mel off the phone I called John Beyer. He had continued to do salvage work for me after the propeller job—if he could survive that, he figured, he could do about anything. Over the course of that time, I had learned that John doesn't sleep. This turned out to be a great asset over the next few years: he can drink and dance and do whatever he does long after everybody else is down and out, and by dawn he's ready to go again.

"Listen, John. Mel Fisher is going to be here in nine hours. Where are we going to find a boat to drag the magnetometer?"

"Why so much warning?"

"Who knows. How about it?"

"Damn. The only guy I know who's still got a boat in the water big enough for that is Stretch Grey."

"What kind of name is Stretch?"

"Big guy," John said. "You don't want to get him angry."

"Look," I said, "give him a call, and tell him we need—"

"Tonight? Barry, he's a lobsterman, he's got to get up before dawn. You want to call him tonight, I'll give *you* the number."

I jotted it down, cut off the line with one finger, then dialed. The digital clock on the shelf over my desk said 12:10.

The phone rang three times before someone picked up the receiver.

A long moment passed.

"Who the hell is this?"

"Stretch? Barry Clifford. John Beyer gave me your number—he said I might be able to charter your boat."

Another long pause.

"What time is it?"

I began to have the distinct feeling I had made a mistake. I gave him the time.

A grunt.

Then a growl.

The line went dead.

Seven o'clock the next morning I tried again, worried he'd already be out of the house. This time he talked, at least.

"You want to go fishing?"

"Not exactly. I want to drag some equipment."

"Look, I'm sorry to disappoint you, but I make my living off that boat. Maybe some afternoon next week I'll be free. If you don't find somebody else, give me a call."

"Wait a minute," I said before he could hang up. "It has to be today. Today and tomorrow. I'll charter the boat by the day."

"What kind of equipment is this?"

I could feel the hook sinking in. "A magnetometer. It's designed to—"

"I know what a magnetometer is." Then: "I'll meet you at the dock."

As it turned out, we never got to the water that day. It quickly became clear that Mel had a party-time attitude toward the whole business. He was a sight: golden red and weather-beaten from years on the water, soft in the belly from a few too many rum and Cokes. He arrived in Puritan country wearing around his neck an authentic "royal strike" coin he said was worth $100,000.

Fay Feild, tall and thin, wore his own gold coin along with a tweed hat and long tweed overcoat. Riding along with them was a fellow they had picked up in Boston, a potential investor.

After all he had lost, Mel was so happy to have won the *Margarita* case that he didn't want to work. He wanted to talk. He talked all day; he was still talking that night, when we went out to dinner at Provincetown's Red Inn, a quaint old building with rose bushes climbing over it. The restaurant, which looked over the water, drew a Sunday crowd, quiet people in sweaters.

After we ordered, Mel excused himself, saying he needed something from the car. Fay and Beyer and the investor and I made small talk about the cape.

We heard Mel return the same time everyone else did. Just inside the door, he had dropped a gold bar. Next we heard the sound of fifty people choking on their chowder; they eyes bugged out of their heads like something in a cartoon.

Fay Feild shook his head. He had been watching the Mel Fisher show for years.

"Sorry, honey," Mel said to the waitress. "This gold is so heavy. You want to carry that for me?" He handed the girl a solid gold chain.

By the time he unloaded his pockets, Mel laid maybe half a million dollars of gold and jewelry on the table. The potential investor was all but writing a check.

All of this explains why, for perhaps the first time in his life, Stretch Grey drew no attention when he entered a room.

I didn't see him—I felt his presence. When I looked away from the gold I saw one of the largest people I've ever seen in my life. Stretch is six ten and weighs three hundred pounds. I later learned he moved to the cape when, as a doorman at a bar in Newport, he punched a rowdy fisherman and knocked him unconscious—for a week.

"Holy hell," Stretch said admiringly. "Who robbed the bank?"

After the introductions, Mel launched into a speech.

"Gold," he said, drawing the word out, forming it with his mouth, "is the quickest path to wealth, the quickest way to power. It's a pure energy source. There are other forms of money—silver, copper, gemstones, paper dollars—but none of them have the aura of gold. You have to work to get it, whether you dig it from the ground or recover what others have lost. But once you've got the taste for going after it, you'll never be able to punch a clock or save for your retirement again. You'll be a treasure hunter for the rest of your life, and everyone who works with you will come down with treasure fever, too. But let me tell you something." He ignored the others, narrowing in on me.

"Barry, I can tell this much—you're going to find it. You've got the passion, the determination. I don't know how much is down there, but you're going to get plenty, and so will everyone around you. A guy like you, all you need is manpower and the right equipment." He leaned back.

For a minute I thought everyone in the restaurant was going to run out into the night and dive in the water. Mel's pitch was that polished.

In contrast, the work we did over the next few days was anticlimactic. That was something else Mel knew that I was beginning to understand: even when you're searching for something rare and exotic, something beautiful and valuable, a lot of the hunt itself is just plain frustration and hard work.

The next morning Fay, an electronics expert, set up the magnetometer. While we hooked it up and dropped it into the water, he connected a strip-chart recorder in the cabin.

A magnetometer is a large, bullet-shaped—and very expensive—device that registers the earth's magnetic field. Measuring magnetism is useful because old ships contain a good bit of iron—cannon,

cannon balls, anchors—and the presence of any ferrous metal alters the magnetic field. So while the magnetometer won't detect gold or silver, it can tell you where there's an unnatural amount of metal.

The magnetometer provides a constant readout: a pen on the strip chart inside the cabin draws a line on a continuously-moving roll of paper. The line isn't perfectly straight, but you watch for anomalies, or "hits": the needle jumps. The denser the metal, and the greater the concentration, the greater the hit.

The magnetometer sensor has to be towed along straight lines only thirty to fifty feet apart at a steady speed. Also, the mag can give false or unreliable readings, so you need to be aware of the tendencies of the particular meter you're using. Every time the chart recorded a hit, Fay would note our Loran coordinates, which boat and ship navigators receive by radio, and mark our place on the map.

Over the next three days, starting at dawn and going until dark, we dragged the sensor over a three or four mile area. It was costing me a lot of my savings from construction and salvage work to rent the boat and the equipment to pay Mel and Fay for their time, and I quickly realized it was going to take much longer to cover the entire target area carefully, back and forth, making sure we stayed on course. As long as we kept watching the chart, we shouldn't miss. But if we veered off course just once—missing a swath of our site, or steering off at an angle—the sensor might never pass over the *Why-dah*'s cannon. And searching the ocean isn't like mowing your lawn; you can't look out and see where you've already been.

During the course of those three days we recorded dozens of hits.

Mel said, "There's definitely a wreck down there—maybe several."

Knowing very well that this area is referred to as "the graveyard," with more than six thousand shipwrecks, I concurred with Fisher's obvious conclusion. Still, the number of hits did seem encouraging. Even though it was November, I put on the old wet suit I had brought along and went over the side.

The water hit me like a snowbank. After catching my breath, I worked my way down. The water wasn't deep, but visibility was no more than a few feet. Hovering over the bottom, I turned a slow circle with my hands, then swam in the direction of what I told myself was a murky shadow. But nothing was down there. All I saw was sand, sand, and more sand.

Back on deck, while I toweled off, Mel said the obvious again. "You're going to have to blow some holes."

To blow holes underwater I was going to need propwash divertors, also known as mailboxes. Mailboxes are simply huge metal elbows that slip over the propellers of a twin-screw boat. You anchor the boat at three points and position it over the area you want to excavate. That's a tricky maneuver, both because of the precision required and because, like Bellamy's double-anchoring in the face of the storm, it leaves the boat susceptible to the surf. After anchoring you start the engine, and when the propellers are engaged the mailboxes force a stream of water into the sand, blowing a pit about eight feet wide at the bottom and up to fifteen feet deep. The concept is simple, but it was going to take a lot of practice to get it just right.

In the cabin, Fay said, "It's tempting to go after the big ones. Remember, the hit won't be as strong if the iron is buried, or if it's old. The biggest hit you get will probably be an anchor somebody lost last month."

He could say whatever he wanted. If that needle jumped off the chart again, I was going back in.

By the time Mel and Fay left, I had made a shopping list. For starters, I needed a boat strong enough to pull the sensor and maneuver, one with a cabin large enough for the electronics and maps. I needed a magnetometer of my own, a Loran receiver, and metal detectors to help us determine how deeply metal was buried.

I had known I'd need good divers, but now I knew I needed someone smart and patient to run the magnetometer—Beyer would leap at the opportunity, and he had a good head for math—and an experienced, reliable helmsman.

As we unloaded the boat the last day, a shadow stretched over me.

"You looking for help?" Stretch said.

Like everyone on the cape who works on the water, he had spent long hours contemplating the hundreds of wrecks lying somewhere beneath him, and he had heard of Mel and Fay.

"I might be." I laughed. "You don't even know what we're doing out here."

"You're going for the *Whydah.*"

I gathered up my wet suit and turned, not saying yes, not saying no.

"I've got a wife and little boy to feed," he said. "But if you're going for the *Whydah*, I want in."

"You make a good living with the lobsters?"

"Not bad."

I gave the deck a glance to make sure we hadn't left anything behind.

"You're willing to give that up for a year?"

"You couldn't keep me away," Stretch said.

Then: "My wife is going to kill me."

In November 1982 the Board of Underwater Archaeological Resources granted me a temporary permit, good for twelve months, to investigate an area precisely defined in my request.

Specifically, they gave me a reconnaissance permit, issued "for the non-disruptive inspection and identification of underwater archaeological resources . . . characterized by minimal site disturbance." I could look, but I couldn't touch. After I obtained further evidence proving the shipwreck was the *Whydah*, the board said, I could apply for an excavation permit "to uncover and/or remove underwater archaeological resources through the use of disruptive investigation techniques." So while I had gotten a permit, I wasn't sure it would do me a lot of good; it didn't seem likely I'd come across a plank that said "Whydah" while I was diving. I'd also have to issue monthly reports and a comprehensive report at the end of the year. Then, if I wanted to continue searching, I'd have to reapply.

Established in 1973 as "the sole trustee of the Commonwealth's underwater heritage," the board had been specifically "charged with the responsibility of encouraging the discovery and reporting, as well as the preservation and protection, of underwater archaeological resources." I couldn't see that they were encouraging me; their requirements made it virtually impossible truly to "discover" anything. They felt they had to be careful to preserve "cultural resources" for the enrichment of the general public, but those resources weren't going to enrich anybody as long as they were buried.

If I didn't find the *Whydah*, one of two things was likely to happen: either someone else would come along and be discouraged by the same nearly unsatisfiable restrictions, or eventually some university or foundation would take on the task, spending years fulfilling all the board's archaeological requirements behind closed doors. Science is necessary, and politics are unavoidable, but professionals in both fields aren't known for their sense of adventure. When Rob McClung and I explored those old ghost towns in Colorado, we had seen a lot of damage that had been done by other so-called explorers: graffiti, broken glass, evidence of stolen fixtures and furniture. Underwater, historical artifacts have to be protected from the same kind of vandals, the sort of people who take what they want with no regard for preservation—but the state archaeological board seemed prejudiced against *all* private salvors.

At the same time, it struck me that the Commonwealth of Massachusetts was more than a little greedy. The law mandated that all treasure had to be sold once the final report was accepted by the board—and that the state was entitled to 25 percent of the value of any treasure or artifacts recovered in its jurisdiction. When I learned that, I knew how those Cape Codders felt when Southack placed his ad telling them to turn over everything they had found. I was the one who would be paying for the entire expedition, and while I had no idea how much it was finally going to cost, I knew it was going to be a lot. And American admiralty law, as opposed to the British law of Southack's day, basically says that the first person who finds an abandoned shipwreck is entitled to keep it. All of it.

I explained this to Allan Tufankjian.

"You know," he said, "Massachusetts won't be the only ones to want a cut of the action. If you're right about this, people are going to be crawling out of the woodwork. You're going to get phone calls from people claiming to be Sam Bellamy's illegitimate descendants."

Neither one of us said anything for a moment. I don't know what he was doing on the other end of the phone, but I was looking at that quotation from Edward Snow tacked to the wall over my desk. Even if I found the treasure, the blue suits would be waiting on shore, holding out their hands.

"I feel like David," I must have said, because Allan asked David who.

"Like David against Goliath."

"You should be so lucky," Allan said. "He won, remember?"

On November 22 we filed suit in the United States District Court in Boston, laying claim to everything we might find. Cape Cod is small; everyone had heard about what was going on. Some people might have looked down at the ground and scuffled their feet and talked about hoping to get lucky, but I'm not that type. I said I had found the *Whydah*, and that got some attention.

So two days later, when John Beyer and I drove up to Wellfleet, we were met by a deputy United States Marshal, park rangers from the Cape Cod National Seashore, and a crowd of television and newspaper reporters. Stretch couldn't make it, so we didn't have a boat. I had come down with a cold after diving in my wet suit when Mel and Fay had come up, so while the reporters worked me over, Beyer swam out fifteen hundred feet in an old diving suit. It was ripped, but we had stopped at a hardware store in town and patched it with electrician's tape.

John anchored a buoy. He attached our permit and an order of the court, both in a waterproof pouch, saying I was guardian of the wreck until title was awarded. Then he put up what was, in essence, a no trespassing sign, warning anybody who thought they'd nose around that they would be fined and/or imprisoned.

When he got back, John handed me a mesh bag of gold coins.

"Beginner's luck," he said, shivering in the breeze.

I passed the coins around to the reporters, who peeled off the foil and ate the chocolate.

"Come back next year," I told them. "Then they'll be real."

When they left, we carried the diving equipment back up to John's car.

"They liked the candy thing."

I sneezed. "Reporters are just like anybody else. You make their job easier, they'll treat you right. How'd the suit hold up?"

"It leaks." He shut the trunk, still toweling his hair with one hand. "Are you going to buy new ones?"

"I guess I have to." We got into the car.

"You should get those dry suits. They're expensive, but you can dive a lot longer."

"I know," I said. "And masks. And tanks. And a compressor."

I sneezed again. I felt like I was coming down with pneumonia, and there was plenty of work to do over the winter before we could even begin to dive. But at last we had staked our claim to the *Whydah*. Now all I needed was a quarter million dollars.

On Christmas Day I got a call from Rob McClung. He and I had stayed close over the years, even though he was out west. Now the chief of police in Aspen, he had become friends with Arnold Schwarzenegger and the other glitterati who had bought property there in the seventies and early eighties.

After we caught up on each other, he told me why he was calling. "Do you remember we agreed to rescue each other from normalcy whenever we got the chance?"

"I'm listening."

"I need rescuing." His marriage was on the rocks and he had a high tension job. "Barry, I want to help you go after the *Whydah*."

Apparently, news travels fast. "What? Do you want to be a diver?"

"I just want in. Diver, whatever."

"Well, I've got to get investors, too. There's no telling how much this is going to cost before we're done." I gave him an idea of what we needed. I could tell he was surprised, but Rob would never admit to being caught off guard.

"I'll talk to some people." Rob even sounds like a cop; he's all authority. "By the time I'm done, they'll be fighting each other for the opportunity." He laughed. "Barry, this is great. I've been waiting to do something like this my whole life."

"This isn't kid's stuff," I told him. "We need to ante up before we start to play. Talk it up with your buddies out there."

Rob was right: this was exactly the sort of thing we had been looking for in college. If all those guys were still in decent shape, and even half as crazy as they had been, I'd have the beginnings of the perfect crew.

That winter, when I wasn't thinking of ways to raise money, I spent long hours applying the results of the partial mag survey to the charts I had at home. Each hit had to be represented by size, Loran coordinates, and the water depth so we wouldn't waste time in the spring surveying the same area. It was tedious work, gathering the data gleaned at sea, poring over it, laying chart over chart, endlessly interpreting.

Late one morning I called out to Birgitta. The kids were in school; I had just heard the teapot whistle in the kitchen.

"What is it?" she said.

I hurried in. "You'll never believe it—one of the strongest hits on the mag survey is at the exact spot I had triangulated from Southack."

"Do you want something hot to drink?"

Everybody has moments that are frozen in memory: snapshots you always carry with you. That's one of mine. Birgitta was standing by the stove, her hips against the counter, leaning back just a little, holding a white and black mug. She hadn't taken a drink yet; the tea was still steaming, clouding up around her face. And the look in her eyes said that if she never heard another word about Southack, mag hits, or the *Whydah*, it would be too soon.

Over the years I convinced a tremendous number of people to believe in my search—everyone from Stretch and Beyer to high rollers and, eventually, the state board—but the person physically closest to me finally didn't care. Birgitta had said that if it took me four years, she'd be waiting for me when I got back. But that was part of the problem; Birgitta saw the search as a long trip, as if I were abandoning the family. The prospect of finding the treasure was exciting, but distant to her, something that might possibly happen far in the future, after we had run through all our savings and gone into debt. In the meantime, she had to live with me, and I was a man possessed.

. . .

Allan drew up papers for a company to be called Maritime Underwater Surveys. We would sell stock, and eventually the company would fund not only the *Whydah*, but whatever other projects I developed afterward. In the meantime, Rob called with an incredible report.

First he had contacted a friend of his, a long-haired judge in Crested Butte named John Levin. Levin was on the board of directors of the Bank of Telluride, located in a booming little ski town. He in turn called one of his fellow directors, a ski enthusiast and real estate developer named Mickey Salloway. Salloway then called his friend and business colleague Bob Lazier. Lazier was a remarkable man: he had grown up in a Minneapolis orphanage, but now he was one of the main developers of Vail. According to Rob, he was worth $25 million.

"These are our kind of guys," Rob said. "They're always looking for an adventure. And they could finance this thing with their spare change."

I wondered whether they'd be as interested in prim New England as they were in the Colorado boomtowns. If these guys had real money, they were used to hearing all kinds of pitches; to them, I was just some sailor from Cape Cod with a crazy idea. Still, I didn't waste any time packing my bag.

On New Year's Eve Rob and John Levin and I drank and talked. We had a good enough time, but the only thing on my mind was the presentation I would give the next day.

"A toast," Levin said at one point, raising his glass. "To finding the *Whydah*."

I raised my glass, smiled, and thought, To financing the *Whydah*.

When I finally got to bed that night I couldn't sleep. Whenever I convinced myself the presentation would go smoothly, I started thinking about the *Islander* case. I had to be back in Massachusetts for a court hearing on the fourth, and as I lay there I kept thinking that if some crazy judge bought the Steamship Authority's story

The legend of the *Whydah* will be preserved in a museum dedicated to the pirates, where future generations can eye treasure hunter Barry Clifford's pirate booty. *Lynn Sugarman, Art and Antiques*

Barry Clifford and Stretch Gray surrounded by treasure on the deck of the *Vast Explorer II*. *Bill Dibble, Maritime Explorations, Inc.*

A typical day on site, November 1984. John Beyer helps a diver onto the *Vast*. Barry Clifford (in the red jacket) talks to one of the archaeological crew as Stretch towers over working divers. Financier Bob Lazier peruses operations from the flying bridge. Water pumps through a sluice and drains overboard. *Maritime Explorations, Inc.*

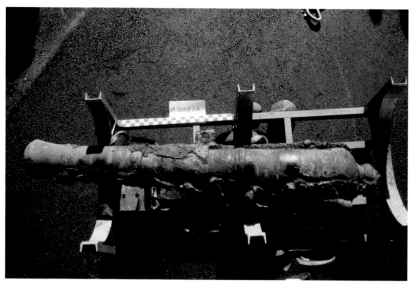

This three-pounder cannon, with wood tompion plugging its muzzle, is probably loaded. The pirates had coated it with pitch or tar, which most likely aided its preservation under water. Of the thirty cannons on the *Whydah*, two were recovered by Southack, twenty-seven have been recovered by maritime explorers. The last cannon remains on site, concreted to the ship's stove under heavy sand cover. *The Whydah Joint Venture*

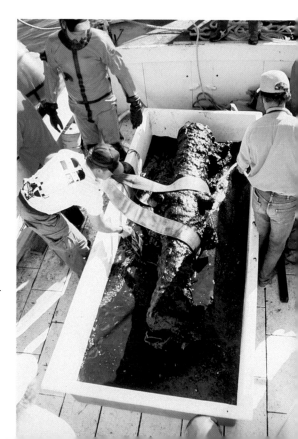

Todd Murphy unstraps a cannon just raised from the site as Stretch looks on. Concreted cannons were covered in wet burlap on board the ship until the crew returned to the lab, where the cannons were placed in light electrolyte baths the crew called "cannon coffins." *Maritime Explorations, Inc.*

Collage of African Akan jewelry: gold ingot, piece of eight, and man's ring. The ring bears the cryptic inscription, TEYE
BA
on the outside, and W*F*S* on the inside. The only ring salvaged from the *Whydah*, it was discovered in a small concretion at the stern and probably belonged to an officer. *The Whydah Joint Venture*

Three hundred to four hundred fragments of Akan jewelry, a major archaeological find, were brought up from the *Whydah* site. Broken into pieces for trading purposes, this jewelry links the *Whydah* to its original service as a merchant slaver. *The Whydah Joint Venture*

These brass ounce weights are nested scale receptacles to measure gold. Graded in Troy ounces, they measured amounts ranging from 1 dram (16 drams make 1 ounce Troy) to 4 ounces. Each receptacle doubled the weight of the next lesser. *The Whydah Joint Venture*

Barry Clifford comes upon gold and silver coins as he investigates a pit blown by a mailbox. More than 8,000 Spanish coins, along with a handful of English, French, and Scottish mints, scattered the entire length of the wreck site and were salvaged by hand, hydraulic dredge, and airlift dredge. *Maritime Explorations, Inc.*

Silver *reales* were produced by cutting bars into roughly circular shapes which were then imprinted with marks that included dates and mint marks from Bolivia, Peru, Colombia, and Mexico. A piece of 8 *reales* weighed about 27 grams of silver and was worth 6 shillings in 1717. Eight *real* coins recovered from the wreck measured 25 grams due to underwater corrosion.

Less common than coins, gold *ingot* is a finger bar weighing approximately 379 grams. Pirates broke the bars by weight for division between the pirate crew and used the pieces for trading.

Nine gold *escudos* were taken from the site. As gold does not deteriorate under water, the weight of these rare coins is virtually unchanged. *Marian Roth*

Gold Escudos

Gold Ingot

Silver Reales (various denominations)

(ABOVE, LEFT) Barry and Rob McClung at the lab with the ship's bell, shortly after its discovery. *Rick Friedman, Black Star*

(ABOVE, RIGHT) The bell, now on display at the Provincetown Museum, rests in a sodium carbonate bath designed to remove sodium chloride from the concretion. Concretions remain around the brass bell's wooden yoke and iron clapper. *Marian Roth*

Three feet of silk ribbon was found knotted and tied around the handle of a pistol in concretion. Pirates often used ribbon to tie the pistols around their necks and to improve their grip on the gun's handle. Since it is remarkable to recover organic material, the ribbon had to be cleaned very carefully. The painstaking process, which involved some electrolysis while the ribbon was still in the concretion, and work with a small pneumatic drill, took about four weeks. It took about three more weeks to remove the ribbon from the pistol. *The Whydah Joint Venture*

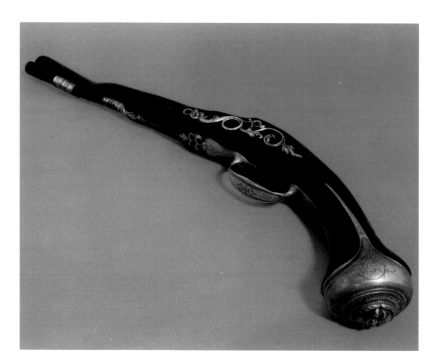

This pistol, shown in concretion and restored, is probably of French design and is fashioned from North American black walnut. It was wrapped in the silk ribbon illustrated in photograph 13, and fitted into a hemp-cloth holster. Remnants of the barrel hold two lead shot, 15 mm each. This "fancy" pistol with ornate brass scrollwork was found at the *Whydah*'s stern and probably belonged to an officer, maybe to Bellamy himself. *The Whydah Joint Venture*

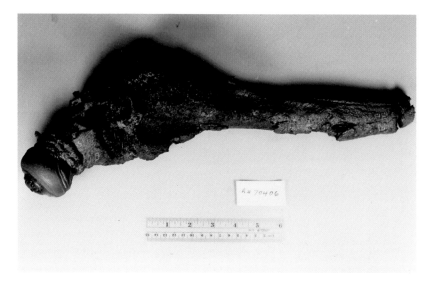

Artist's conception of swashbuck-
ling captain "Black Sam" Bellamy.
Ron Fowler's portrait incorporates
personal items recovered from the
wreck of the *Whydah* galley.
Marian Roth

Barry Clifford, a modern-day
pirate prince, on the deck of the
Vast Explorer II with Heidi Pearl.
Maritime Explorations, Inc.

about me donating my services, I was going to be out all the money I had planned to use for the *Whydah* plus Allan's fees.

I punched the pillow. We would win the court case.

But then I heard Birgitta's voice, saw the way she had looked at me in the kitchen. As if that wasn't enough, I had a pinched nerve in my neck, so when I wasn't tossing over the *Whydah* or the *Islander,* my twitching shoulder kept me awake.

The next morning I was wound up. On the ride to Vail one voice was saying: *This is only the beginning.* The other voice said: *This is it, pal. All or nothing.*

That first formal meeting, if you could call it that, took place in Lazier's $6 million penthouse apartment atop the Tivoli Lodge in Vail. The penthouse has one huge room with three sofas and long windows that look out onto the mountains. It says something about Lazier, one of the most content people I've ever met, that he used that space as his office, his relaxation room, and his children's playroom—for him, those functions weren't separate.

After Rob introduced Lazier and Salloway, we went through a few minutes of the kind of introductory chit-chat that drives me up the wall. Then Rob bailed me out.

"Are you going to make us wait forever?" he said. "Tell us your secrets."

Sitting there on a plush sofa, looking out on the snow-covered mountains, I caught my breath. Mel Fisher had been preaching to the converted; I had to sell the treasure hunt to this room full of businessmen.

"Rich with two hundred and sixty-six years of folklore, the *Whydah* is the most written-about shipwreck in American waters during the eighteenth century. Initially this would appear as a great aid to a salvor. However, the copious legends make for something of a jigsaw puzzle, albeit one in which some of the pieces overlap, and others don't belong at all."

I was nervous; I could hear it in my voice. It all sounded too rehearsed, like somebody else was talking.

"Captain Cyprian Southack was commissioned by Governor Shute to recover the treasure. He was a cartographer, so he was meticulous; he detailed his failure in his log and in his letters to the governor. After identifying the site of the wreck, I see why he failed: he faced breakers only five hundred yards off shore and forty degree water. They didn't have wet suits in 1717."

Levin smiled politely, but Salloway and Lazier were expressionless; either I was losing them or they were keeping their cards close to their chests.

"Using a magnetometer, a specialized sort of metal detector, we've identified the location of over one hundred metal objects buried in the sand." That much came from my survey with Mel and Fay. "A group of these objects appear to weigh one thousand to two thousand pounds, which is what we'd expect the cannons to weigh. None of the anomalies is attached by metal cable, which indicates an early wreck. Two locals collected dozens of coins on the beach nearby during the 1930s; I've personally found pipe stems, earthenware, and bronze chisel point nails of the period near the site."

Listening to myself, wondering whether I'd write me a check for $250,000, I realized what was wrong.

I wasn't telling the story.

Uncle Bill, wherever he was, had to be shaking his head. This wasn't what had captured my imagination all those years ago; I was trying to sell this as if I were some kind of stockbroker. If Bill had been here he'd be tapping his cigarette into the cuff of his jeans, taking his time, sinking the hook into these guys until they couldn't tear it loose.

So I backed up. I told them how Sam Bellamy had started as a sailor. I threw in Maria Hallett for romance, Blackbeard for recognition. I told them about the Silver Plate Fleet and the vote of Bellamy's crew to go on the account. I told them about Thomas Davis and Thomas South, about the *Sultana* and then the slave ship laden with gold, the *Whydah*. Without realizing I had memorized it, I launched into Bellamy's famous "I am a free prince" speech, the one he had used to defend everything he believed in.

The wind and rain pounded Bellamy off the *Whydah*'s rigging and into the sea the night of the wreck, but I concentrated on the words *gold, silver, treasure.*

"It's a risk. But something you can tell your grandchildren about. You have the chance to be the first ever to discover an authentic, documented pirate ship."

For one endless moment, no one said a word.

Then the room exploded with questions.

Levin: "How do you know Bellamy was a real man, not some mythical character?"

"The court records are filled with evidence. Bellamy was as real as the six of us."

Lazier: "All you've found are some pipe stems and signs of metal. What makes you so sure the majority of the treasure hasn't already been found?"

"What came ashore were floatables, like sails and wooden masts. The heavier 'riches and guns' sank in the sand while Southack watched. If you add up the accounts of the treasure on board, even if thousands of coins washed ashore, that's still a small percentage of the total."

"Okay," Mickey Salloway said. "Let's assume for a minute that all this gold and silver is down there. Why hasn't somebody else already brought it up?"

If these were the hardest questions they could ask, I thought to myself, I should have enjoyed myself last night.

"The equipment we're using didn't exist before World War II."

But Lazier wasn't finished. "It's going to take a lot of men to do all the work you're talking about. Getting the treasure is one thing; then you've got the lab you say you'll need to restore and preserve artifacts, lab technicians, archaeologists . . . your budget seems unrealistic. A quarter of a million won't even cover salaries."

I saw the trap waiting to snap shut. Rob told me later he thought Lazier was saying I should ask for more; but I knew immediately he was trying to find out how much I meant to pay myself. Those men hadn't made their fortunes by giving money away.

"Until we find the treasure," I told him, "I'm working for free. The divers and crew work in exchange for stock in the company. We'll need to pay outside consultants, those professionals you mentioned, but virtually all the money I'm raising will go toward equipment. We'll be bringing up treasure by the end of the summer."

There I went again; daring myself.

"When you invest in Maritime," I continued, "you aren't just buying a piece of the *Whydah*. This isn't a one-shot deal. There are thousands of wrecks just waiting for someone who's willing to do the historical research and use the right equipment. Ships don't disappear when they sink; they're all sitting on the ocean bottom. I'm not just talking about finding a pirate ship with a wonderful history. This is the beginning of a whole new high-tech treasure-hunting industry."

We talked for a while longer, but Lazier was getting restless. I said something about it being terrible to be cooped up indoors so long in such a beautiful place, and he nearly jumped to his feet.

"Let's take a break," he said. "I'll show you one of my little projects."

Ice and snow covered the streets, but he drove as if it were the middle of summer. When we got to a warehouse he owned, he took us in and showed us a disassembled jet.

"It's a Pinto," he said. "These were used as trainers."

"You're going to sell it?" Rob asked.

Lazier shook his head. "You can't find these anymore. I'm piecing it together from a manual I found. I've spent more than a hundred thousand dollars trying to bring this baby back to life—a hundred thousand too much, as far as my wife is concerned." He grinned. "I plan to use it as a second car."

Before we left he told us he flew and raced cars as a hobby; he'd even won Indy Car Rookie of the Year two years earlier. I started to relax.

We all spent the next few days in Vail. We went skiing. At one point Mickey Salloway and I rode the lift together.

"I'm in," Mickey said. "You know that, right?"

Before I left, Lazier and Salloway gathered some of their friends—investment bankers, industrialists, real estate tycoons, ski bum attorneys, the whole range of intrepid gamblers who inhabit a place like that—and helped sell them on the *Whydah* project. When we were finished, Maritime Underwater Surveys had become Maritime Explorations, a private placement stock company, and we had an initial group of investors. Mickey Salloway's lawyer said he would have the offering ready in two weeks.

I had time to go skiing once more before I left. Racing down the mountain, breathing the crisp air, I felt like nothing could stop me.

◆　◆　◆

My feet touched ground as soon as I got back home. The court case on the *Islander* was postponed for at least a month. Sometimes I thought I'd rather have it over with, whatever the outcome, instead of having to wait.

Pushing that frustration out of my mind, I started spending the money from Colorado. The first item on my list was a dive boat sturdy enough to endure the trip from Provincetown all the way around Race Point to the *Whydah* site thirty-five miles away. That's a rough stretch of water, especially when the tides and currents work against you. A lot of the time she'd have to make the trip twice a day, morning and night, because we couldn't leave her anchored over the site in bad weather. Uncle Bill's partner had drowned going around Race Point. Our budget was tight, but we couldn't cut corners on the dive boat.

Stretch heard that a sixty-five foot naval "sonar chaser" built by Harvey Gammage had been retired from service and put up for sale. Gammage had been a legendary nautical craftsman working out of South Bristol, Maine, and this was the last wooden boat he built. Wood gave the boat character, and it also meant the magnetometer would be able to work efficiently, without the "distraction" of a metal boat. Sonar chasers are used to monitor sonar buoys, which act like underwater microphones, for tracking Russian submarines. Since we were going to be doing some underwater sleuthing our- selves, the Gammage boat sounded perfect.

A twin propeller diesel made from white oak, the *Vast Explorer* had a high mast, a high bow ideal for cutting through choppy water, and a wide afterdeck with plenty of work space. The pilothouse was already filled with navigational equipment, and the radio room, which sat under the mast, directly behind the pilothouse, could serve as our dive shack, where we would stow suits and tanks and elec- tronic gear. The *Vast* had plenty of space for a crew and galley, which was important, as we'd have to be able to live on the boat twenty-four hours a day. Maybe even more important than all of that was the feeling I had when I stood on her deck the first time. She was as strong as a battleship, built with huge timbers and double-planked; she had soul. "This," I told Stretch," "is a good luck boat."

The *Vast* had been named for its previous owner, a corporation that had classified contracts with the U.S. Navy. Stretch pointed out that as long as we were talking about luck, it would be tempting fate to rename her. Ironically, over the next few years people claimed I had named the boat myself in a fit of arrogance. Sometimes it's best to let them think what they want.

I agreed to pay $80,000, or nearly a third of my total budget. On top of that, we still needed to have it refitted and repainted. Gammage said they could do the work by May or June, and when I told them that was too late they said it would go faster—and be cheaper—if the people who were going to be using the boat were up there, telling them exactly what was needed and helping with the finishing touches.

I explained this to Stretch, Beyer, and Todd Murphy. Murphy was a young diver I knew. A Green Beret in the reserves, he was getting a degree in Exercise Physiology at the University of Connecticut. A hard worker, he kept himself in great shape. He was clean cut and athletic without being muscle bound. I told the three of them what Gammage had told me, and that I wasn't able to offer much in the way of payment aside from shares of stock. But they believed; to them, stock in the treasure none of us had seen yet was worth more than a salary. We went to South Bristol together and got a good deal on a rented house the locals claimed was haunted.

After getting them situated, I came back to find a smaller boat to transport us to and from the *Vast* when she was anchored at the site. I found a Boston Whaler I named the *Crumpstey* after Captain Andrew Crumpstey, the master of the *Mary Anne*, who died aboard the *Whydah*. As long as we were going to be dealing with ghosts, we might as well get them on our side.

My plan was to have the *Crumpstey* tie up at Nauset Harbor near Orleans, only six nautical miles to the southwest of my permit area. Nauset Harbor is the long, meandering cove Southack and his crew ended up in after slogging their way across the cape. Getting in and out of the harbor is supremely tricky because it's impassable at low tide and full of shifting sandbars. When I asked Stretch if he thought it was a bad idea to work out of the harbor, he said, "There's plenty of water there, it's just spread out real thin." Not only that, but where the mouth empties into the Atlantic there's a line of breakers doing their damnedest to crush you. The whaler proved unsinkable, and even when we took breakers straight over the pilothouse, it never flipped over.

There was no way to save money on the magnetometer, the mailboxes, the Aquapulse underwater metal detectors, or the Loran, and when I had gotten them I had run through most of my budget. I purchased four wet suits instead of the more expensive dry suits; at least they weren't taped together. Instead of buying a compressor to refill our tanks on board the ship, I decided we could drive to Hyannis every night and refill them there. We'd get in and out of the water from atop the mailboxes instead of using a ladder. Underwater, we'd communicate with special slates instead of radio equipment. A lot of the crew would have to use their own gear. I had no other choice.

In February the *Islander* hearing finally came before the court; I won, but the Steamship Authority immediately filed another appeal. I felt like a character from a Dickens novel, going to court over this one case for the rest of my life.

I did some skiing, some days for hours at a time. I especially enjoyed the smell of the rain in the fir trees and the peculiar smell of melting snow on a warm winter day, tiny streams beginning to flow down the mountain. It helped to get outside and forget about the fact that Mickey Salloway's lawyer still hadn't finished the paperwork for the offering, which meant I didn't actually have any of the money I was spending. On top of that, Mel Fisher stopped returning my calls. He was having so much trouble with the state and the national park that when I suggested using Fisher's archaeologist, Duncan Mathewson, on the *Whydah*, the Massachusetts board threatened to revoke my permit. In my enthusiasm with Fisher's much publicized successes, I hadn't anticipated all of the traps in the academic world that had already ensnared him. Like it or not, I found myself about to be thrown into the same lot with Fisher. Over a year went by before I realized Mel had done all the work on the cape he was going to do with me; that was the last I saw or heard of him. I've tried to distance myself from that initial association ever since.

By the end of March I was completely out of money. When

Birgitta saw the kinds of checks I was writing, knowing we couldn't possibly keep covering them, she saw me as a traitor. In her mind, I was deliberately endangering her and Jenny, Barry Jr., and Brandon. What she couldn't understand was my confidence. I knew—not hoped, but *knew*—I would be running my hands through the *Whydah*'s treasure by the end of the year.

Instead of believing, Birgitta asked the practical question. When was all this money coming?

I tried to reassure her, but I wanted to know the answer myself. While Levin, Salloway, and Lazier still talked a good game on the phone, I couldn't help but wonder if there was something they weren't telling me. They went back and forth about paperwork, complicated negotiations between lawyers . . . I wanted to be able to drop a gold bar on the carpet in Levin's penthouse, but until I saw some money, there would be no gold bars to drop.

I did a lot of running, which helped psychologically and physically. One day I got a late start and ended up running in the dark; I forced myself to finish by invoking the ghosts of the *Whydah*. But Southack had gone door to door; Bellamy went ship to ship. I was just running in circles. The next morning I flew back to Colorado.

In *The Treasure of the Sierra Madre,* Howard, the old man who convinces the two down-and-out-Americans to try their luck searching for gold in the hills of Mexico, tells them,

> Going with a partner or two is dangerous. All the time murder's lurking about. Hardly a day passes without quarrels—the partners accusing each other of all sorts of crimes, and suspecting whatever you do or say.

He goes on to say the trouble only starts once you've hit it rich—but in our case, just the thought of big money was putting friendships to the test. John Levin, the judge, whom Rob McClung considered his friend, asked me if he'd have the power to hire and fire people working on the project. Hesitant, I told him yes, I guessed he'd have some influence in determining whom we hired.

He said, "I want to fire Rob."

My jaw must have hung halfway to the floor. We hadn't spent a day on the water, and already I was faced with my first case of mutiny.

"He's power hungry," Levin told me.

"There's a lot of money at stake here," I said. "Everyone's going to have his moment of paranoia. If Rob gets out of line, we can do something about it when it happens. But at this point I'm trying to assemble the best crew I can get, and Rob's a part of it. You'd be shooting yourself in the foot."

Levin calmed down. By the time I left, everyone seemed to be on an even keel, and they assured me the check was all but in the mail.

I chose to take them at their word; there was more shopping to do before we'd be ready to get to work. Everyone was going to need housing as close to the permit area as possible. I had told a friend of mine, a realtor, that I needed two houses near Nauset Harbor, one for me and my top command and one for the rest of the crew. We had already chosen the crew's house, an admittedly spartan affair, which they immediately nicknamed The Barracks.

When I got back from Denver the broker took me to a house he thought I could use. A stately nineteenth-century home surrounded by generous maples and birches, it came to be known as the Captain's House, both because I lived there and because it was filled with nautical knickknacks and old family paintings. The sort of house only a Cape Codder could fully appreciate, it still had the feeling of all the people who had lived there. But what made it perfect was this: the house sat next to the swampy remains of Jeremiah's Gutter.

Two hundred and sixty-six years earlier, Southack had rowed through my back yard. Now I was about to finish the job he had started.

CLAIM JUMPERS

WORKING UNDER WATER . . . IS LIKE working under water. It's slow and dangerous.

In February the board attached nine conditions to my permit, including requests for all sorts of information about personnel, data on every dive we made, and permission to come to the site whenever they wanted. I gave them as much as I could, which ate up plenty of time, and questioned some of their demands. In contrast to what I had told the Colorado group, my proposal to the board said the entire operation—from our initial search of the site to the day every last piece of treasure was identified and cataloged—would last four to five years. It would take a long time to satisfy all of their requirements both on the water and on land, and if I underestimated how long the job would take, everyone—not just the board, but investors, the press, the crew—might run out of patience.

When spring broke on the cape the *Vast* still wasn't fully refitted, but I was desperate to get out of the house, away from the phone. On a brisk, breezy morning in May, the core of the crew gathered at Nauset Harbor.

Our immediate goal was to learn the trick of getting the twenty-five-foot *Crumpstey* in and out of the inlet. I had driven past it, but now I was astounded at the intensity of the breakers, and the narrow channel that led through them. It was going to take practice to keep from running aground, and a little luck wouldn't hurt.

Beyer said, "This is insane."

"It's the closest safe mooring," I reminded him.

"It would be easier to drive a car through there than steer a boat."

"If you can't do it . . ."

"I'll do it," he said. "Still, it's crazy."

One of the more enjoyable jobs that winter had been contacting the old friends who stood on the *Crumpstey* now, talking about the season ahead. Bill Dibble, an old buddy I hadn't seen in fifteen years, had flown up in April. He had always been an all-around success: a good student, a football player, and a great friend. After serving in Vietnam as a Marine fighter pilot, he became a photographer. Although he seemed satisfied with the way things had worked out, he didn't have to think twice about putting his career on hold to hunt for treasure.

"You sure you're up for it?" I asked him. Bill had let himself go a little, and the currents offshore were no place for an out-of-shape swimmer.

"Look, Cliff. You don't have to tell me to get my act together— the next time I see you, I'll be ready."

If he wasn't quite back to his old form that first day in May, I could tell he was working on it. Bill was going to be fine.

Dibble said, "If it doesn't get any warmer than this, we're going to need an icebreaker, not a whaler."

Trip Wheeler told him, "Up here, this is a heat wave."

Just from talking on the phone I had been able to tell Trip hadn't gone soft since college. In March I told him when we expected to have the *Vast,* and he said he'd be there. I hung up realizing he hadn't asked about salary, lodging, his specific responsibilities, or any of that. Trip didn't care; he was always up for something new.

What surprised me was when I called Rob, telling him to get his plane ticket. He was uncharacteristically subdued.

"It's too much to get into. I'll tell you, though—I've got to get out of here."

"There'll be plenty to keep you busy. A newspaper up here quoted somebody who said the treasure could be worth $400 million. We're going to have every two-bit crook in the country waiting at the dock."

"Diver, security guard, you name it. I'll be there."

As we headed back through the inlet, he was as clear-eyed and authoritative as ever.

"Piece of cake," he said. "By June we'll be going through here blindfolded."

Not quite. A week later a breaker smashed our steering, and from then on the trip from the harbor to the permit area turned into a personal challenge. Beyer, Stretch, and I took turns piloting the whaler.

Imagine one of those chamber of commerce advertisements for Cape Cod, the scene tourists and amateur photographers can't resist: early morning sun, brilliant blue sky, rustic boats meeting their perfect reflections on the water's surface. The local fishermen quietly anchored in the shoals and channels, clam rakers and men setting nets, water softly slapping the shore. We'd ease our way past, waving, calling hellos—and then, as soon as we cleared the breakers, open up the engines, roaring out to the site.

It was five miles each way, and we made a lot of trips shuttling people back and forth; we couldn't afford to waste time. But there were always a few locals who wanted to make a fuss, claiming we ran too fast, or disturbed the fish. Despite my family's history on the cape, to some old-timers I was an outsider. You can imagine what that made the rest of the crew. Wherever we went, people looked at us the way I imagined their ancestors had looked at Southack; they knew what we were doing, didn't want us to succeed, and wouldn't mind if the door hit us on our way out.

Without the *Vast* and the mailboxes we couldn't blow holes, but we had our magnetometer. I explained to the crew that we would continue the mapping, dragging the mag, and anchoring buoys over strong hits. It didn't seem all that exciting, but when the *Vast* came through we'd know the best spots to explore.

By now it was late May. Beyer or Dibble or Charlie Burnham watched the mag readings, the rest of us concentrated on keeping a steady course. Charlie was an old friend of mine from the Vineyard. A Yale graduate and something of a genius with robotics, he just wanted to come along to see what he could learn. A chill wind had us shivering, and a thick fog hung over the boat. Fog on the water doesn't just make it difficult to see; it creates an eerie blanket of isolation. Not knowing what's out there as you're moving makes you more tentative. I was about to say we should head in when Beyer said aloud, really just talking to himself, "There's a big one."

I looked over the side of the *Crumpstey*, thinking it would be a month or more before we'd be able to see what was down there. And that was too long. How much colder and wetter could it be underwater?

"Hold it," I said. As I took off my jacket and shirt, somebody handed me my wet suit. Everyone had been thinking the same thing; they all wanted to dive.

I climbed into the suit, added a lead weight belt, pulled my boots and hood on, slipped into my buoyancy compensator and tank. A little clumsy in all that gear, I sat on the rail, while someone handed me my fins which I pulled on over the booties. I checked the gauges, put the regulator in my mouth, slipped down my mask, and went over and in.

On a perfect day—and there weren't many—visibility off the cape might be twenty feet. That day it was closer to six. I swam down to where I thought the mag had been when it registered the hit, but of course there was nothing sitting out on the sand—I didn't expect it to be that easy. Operating by touch as much as by sight, I dug with my hands.

Whatever was down there, it lay deeper than I could dig. But from then on, we dove. I did a lot of it myself, staying down for forty-five or sixty minutes at a time, going back again and again. We'd stand a much better chance with the *Vast* blowing pits, but I couldn't see any reason to waste the beginning of the season. While we dove, the *Crumpstey* kept going, surveying.

We didn't find any treasure those first few weeks, but we developed a routine. The crew was so small that they'd get us into position, then become the dive crew, then turn back into the boat crew. There was plenty of work to keep everyone busy. We kept the equipment organized, helped each other check and recheck the dive gear, and kept a record of how long each man stayed under water. When you're diving in less than thirty feet you don't have to worry about the bends or any of the other hazards of deep-water diving, but with a maximum water temperature of about sixty degrees, I was concerned about the dangers of exposure. Cold, tired divers meant a cold, tired boat crew at the end of the day, and that meant someone could get hurt.

When I dove, I watched the patterns of the currents. I'd be digging with my hands, hoping to feel something solid, and at the same time thinking, A lot of the treasure has drifted. That close to the beach, the movement of the water isn't consistent; it's affected by wind and waves, tides and currents. The treasure would have spread north and south, which meant we'd need to expand the search to find everything.

Trying to sense the *Whydah,* I realized that Black Sam Bellamy's bones could literally be under my hands; it gave the skull and crossbones new meaning. With every thrust into the sand I reached for the lid of a coffin.

That spring was one of the rainiest in years; I told the crew Bellamy's ghost was taunting us. Anybody who would be put off by a little bad weather didn't deserve the *Whydah.*

One day a bank manager with a touch of thunder in his voice called to tell me a $70,000 check hadn't cleared, which meant most of the checks I had recently written for the company were no good. Then the *Crumpstey*'s starboard engine blew. The day after we had it repaired, Beyer and Charlie Burnham took it out to test the new engine and do some surveying. I talked to Stretch, who was back in Maine, working on the *Vast.*

"She's almost ready for paint," he said. "But we've got to finish up with the generators and the pump. I'd say it'll be another couple of weeks."

The delay wasn't Stretch's fault, but I bitched at him. On land, the bank was coming after my throat; in the water, half the summer had passed without us blowing our first test pit. Five years was starting to feel like an optimistic deadline.

I no sooner hung up then I got a call from Beyer.

"I thought you were at the site."

"That's where we were headed," he said. "Charlie and I found a rock in the channel."

"A big one?"

"I can show it to you if you're interested. Wiped out the propellers." Charlie was always asking to pilot the *Crumpstey;* it finally came out that Beyer had given him his chance, with this result. We later named his discovery Burnham Rock. At the time, though, I wasn't laughing.

"This isn't coincidence," I told John. "This is a curse."

We repaired the *Crumpstey,* and a few days later Mickey Salloway flew in from Colorado like a beaming angel. Together we went to the Barnstable Bank to meet with a very unhappy bank president and vice president.

We waited in the lobby. I told Salloway, "If these guys don't get something from us, they're going to come after my house. Did you bring money?"

"Barry," he started. Then he just smiled. "That's not how this works."

Three hours later we walked out with a certified check for $70,000.

"I almost feel guilty," I told Mickey in the parking lot. "That was like a stickup."

"It's the look in your eyes," he said, "that sound in your voice . . . They were *glad* to fix those checks. They were *honored.*"

The crew for the *Vast*'s journey from South Bristol consisted of Stretch at the helm, Beyer as first mate, and Brad Crosby. A graduate of the Massachusetts Marine Academy, Brad would dive and look after the *Vast*'s engines and electrical systems. They stopped in Fairhaven, where the mailboxes had been constructed, and picked up John Kennedy, Jr., who was between semesters at Brown University.

In the rush to get to the cape, Stretch decided they could take care of a few finishing touches along the way. When Kennedy shook hands and asked, enthusiastically, what he could do, Stretch had him crawl into a dank little section of the stern called the lazaret to paint the rudder posts. The purpose isn't aesthetic but to inhibit rust, which will eventually destroy a boat. The space is cramped—there was no way Stretch could have squeezed in there—so Kennedy was breathing engine fumes and wearing lead paint.

Despite what magazine reporters wanted to believe, Kennedy was just another member of the crew. He didn't expect special treatment and no one gave it to him. Stretch put him to the same sort of test he'd give any potential crew member; the challenge wasn't simply to work in bad conditions, but to do the work well.

Kennedy came out smiling.

Stretch crouched down to look over the result. "Nice job," he said.

I met the *Vast* at Vineyard Haven, anxious to put her to work. It only took a minute, though, to realize something was wrong.

"You guys look like hell. Rough weather?"

"Bad fog," Stretch said cheerfully, "but that's not the problem. We've got ourselves a real puker."

The *Vast* was sturdy, but because of all her high rigging, she rolled with every wave. Virtually everyone got sick on her at one time or another, and when they did, discovered something else: the boat's gunwales were so high you couldn't hang over the side to vomit. The crew took turns spending the eighty-mile trip from Maine practicing what Stretch christened "power-puking": crouching down by one of the scupper holes designed to drain water off the deck and trying to vomit accurately on a rolling ship.

That was the kind of special skill they developed. It wasn't the sort of thing just anyone would appreciate.

At the end of the first week in July 1983, more than the usual number of sunbathers gathered on Marconi Beach to watch an unusual boat flying a black flag. Those who had binoculars recognized the flag as the Jolly Roger and noticed the crew wore matching T-shirts bearing the legend "Whydah Pirates."

Our day actually began on shore, on the shady lawn of the Captain's House, within view of Jeremiah's Gutter. The crew gathered, some sitting on lawn chairs, some on the ground, drinking coffee or gnawing a piece of toast, while I explained the day's plan. As the group grew—eventually there were fifteen to twenty of us on any given day that summer—I could feel their determination. When we were flush we'd all eat breakfast at Captain Elmer's Restaurant and Market, and from the way the regulars watched us, you knew they thought the treasure hunting circus had come to town.

For every disgruntled fisherman who cursed us there were dozens of people curious to find out exactly what we were doing to find the *Whydah* and how we were doing it. Learning our routine, people would intercept us in the morning and ask to come on the boat, along with the newspaper reporters and photographers and sometimes entire television crews. If the *Crumpstey* went close to shore they'd ask whether we had found any pieces of eight, or wooden legs; they'd ask where they could get one of those T-shirts. In all but the worst weather, we worked in front of an audience.

I don't know how productive we looked at a distance during those early days on the *Vast Explorer*, but we spent a lot of our time learning how to use the mailboxes.

When we decided on a hit worth exploring, Todd Murphy swam out and swung the head of the mag sensor around to try to pinpoint the location, then marked the spot with a surface buoy. I'd decide the best direction to face the boat, depending on wind and waves and current, and then we'd begin anchoring.

In most cases we dropped the bow anchor first, backing the *Vast* down. The stern anchors were hauled into position 45 degrees off the stern by one of our utility boats—the *Crumpstey* or an inflatable. The sea constantly shifted the *Vast*, so when the three anchors were set we fine-tuned our position by adjusting the length of the mooring lines. The two stern lines ran on vertical capstans which turned on a rotor. Even using hydraulic power, anchoring accurately could take the better part of an hour.

Each mailbox, or metal elbow, consisted of eight hundred pounds of aluminum. They're attached to the boat by strong hinges, but they have to be lowered very slowly to avoid damage to the stern and propellers. A diver locked them into position and we were ready to start.

When the propellers began turning, forcing water down against the bottom, we'd get a lot of scummy bubbles, sediment, and decaying matter. We listened carefully to the rattling of the mailboxes; atypical sounds meant cracking aluminum. If all went well, after half an hour or so we'd have made a hole the shape of a funnel eight feet in diameter at the bottom sloping up to twelve or sixteen feet. Then we had to wait, sometimes another thirty minutes, for the scum and sand to begin to settle so the divers could see. Because the base of the pit was relatively small, if our calculations were off even by five feet—not much of a margin of error in the ocean—we could completely miss what we were after. The *Vast* couldn't move with the mailboxes over the propellers, so if we were off by much, we'd have to start over. Also, we had to be on constant lookout for rogue waves or changes in the weather; we worked in such shallow water— usually no more than thirty feet—so close to shore, that we could have been swept onto the beach in just a few minutes.

That July it took us anywhere from an hour and a half to two hours to blow a pit where we wanted it. With practice, we cut that in half.

Underwater, there wasn't much to do after blowing the pit but to wait until the sand cleared. As Southack had discovered, the sand off the cape isn't packed solid; it's fluid. You can stick your arm through it. So while it's reasonably easy to dig, once you disturb it—by blowing a hole, for instance—the sand doesn't sit in a nice mound, but instead floats around you. Worse, in July and August we also battled mung weed. Mung is actually an algae that forms dense, dark clumps. It tends to rest along the bottom, but when we disturbed it, it would float around us until it felt like we were in a dark blizzard. When we dug holes, the mung weed would slide down the edges, covering the bottom, eventually settling like a grassy blanket on top of us. Trip Wheeler told a reporter the visibility was best when we had our eyes closed.

We tried to speed up the process by using paddles to fan away sand and debris, and worked to keep from aggravating the problem by restricting our movements inside the pits. If you kicked too hard with your fins, or dug too deeply into the pit wall, you lost visibility again. Our digging was a curious combination of the tremendous force of the propellers and the divers' delicate movements.

Divers were instructed to bring to the surface anything they couldn't positively identify as trash. That kept us from looking at beer bottles, but it meant we spent a lot of time looking at junk metal—everything from nails to what turned out to be an old washing machine motor—trying to guess how old it was or whether it might somehow have been part of the *Whydah*. Toward the middle of the month one of our youngest divers, Scotty Magoun, broke the surface shouting, struggling with something he cradled in both arms, still out of sight. "I found a cannon!"

We all rushed to the rear of the boat. McClung got on his knees and reached down, but as soon as the cylinder came into sight, Todd Murphy shouted, "Drop it!"

"It's the first cannon!" Scotty insisted. One day, in a fit of enthusiasm, I had said that when we found the first cannon I would buy everyone on the crew a new Corvette.

"That's no cannon," Todd told him. "It's a bomb! Get it off of here!"

The Green Beret was right; we had discovered the garbage of Camp Wellfleet, where World War II soldiers honed their skills firing machine guns, launching rockets, and dropping bombs. After that we came across an arsenal of bronze ammunition rounds and dud bombs, called drones, from the target range.

So while the clock ticked on our permit, and our finances gradually disappeared, just out of sight, beneath the sand, bombs were waiting for us.

A few days later Kennedy and Murphy were diving when Kennedy lost his grip on one of our metal detectors. It got caught in a fast current, and that easily it was gone.

"I'm sorry, Barry," Kennedy said after he and Todd finally came back on deck. "If we can take the *Crumpstey* out there," he pointed south, "I'll keep looking."

We searched, but it was lost. With our limited budget, every mistake hurt. The one good thing is that the accident made everyone more careful with equipment.

"Let's not waste the pit, too," I told him. We had blown a deep one, maybe eighteen feet at the center, where we had gotten an unusually large hit on the mag readout. Kennedy wanted to dive again, and I went down with him.

Even in the deep pits there wasn't much room for two divers to maneuver. Any sudden movement could knock away the other diver's mask or mouthpiece, so each of us had to be careful, aware of where the other was searching. We used our diving lights to inspect the floor and walls of the hole, brushing lightly at the sand. I pointed to some spent shells, but we both knew they hadn't been responsible for the strip-chart needle's jump.

I didn't expect to find a chest of gold coins; more likely, we'd locate the wreck by discovering the *Whydah*'s cannons or iron hull fittings. We scoured the pit, but there was no sign of whatever the mag had registered, so either it lay deeper or we had aimed the propellers off center. I reached for the underwater slate attached to my nylon harness and wrote a question mark, then tapped myself on the chest and pointed up. I wanted to see if I could figure out what was wrong. Kennedy nodded, then indicated he'd keep looking.

What happened next helped him forget about the lost metal detector. Almost as soon as I left, he noticed a depression in the pit wall. Checking his compass, he saw the hollow was almost exactly north northeast, a little more than two feet from the bottom. Reaching down, he felt something hard and heavy. Excited, he turned up to see if he could get my attention, and as his fins brushed the wall of the pit, sand started pouring down on top of him from every direction.

"It was like being buried alive," he said. "The first time I tried to kick, it felt as if someone had grabbed my feet." Luckily, he kept his cool; holding his arms to his sides, body rigid, he moved his fins with his feet and ankles, not long leg kicks, and popped out of the pit like a cork.

A diver doesn't have to make a mistake to get into serious trouble. I knew that with as many hours as we would be underwater day after day, month after month, with poor visibility, someone might easily make a misjudgment and come up under the boat, or under the mailboxes—or get swept off in the current. Each man regularly checked his tank harness, his weight belt, his compass, his watch. I established similar routines above the surface, on the *Vast* and the *Crumpstey*.

Leaving Kennedy in the pit, I had broken one of my own rules; after that, we'd always dive in pairs and come up together. Too many things could go wrong too fast.

Just inside the door of the Land Ho, looking for an empty table, I heard my name.

The Land Ho is a wonderful little neighborhood hangout, a restaurant with a bar running along one side and various signs nailed to the walls and beams creating a rustic decor. Tired but freshly showered, I was ready to relax. After we came in from the site I usually swam or ran with a few of the others. Strange as it sounds, swimming in a pond was enjoyable even after a day of diving; without any equipment, we'd jump in and race.

"He's in the wrong place, for one thing," this guy sitting at the bar was saying. By that time I had developed a sixth sense; I knew this was about the *Whydah*.

"They blow through the inlet like they owned the damned world," the man next to him said, holding his beer just short of his mouth. "I'll bet you they give it three more weeks."

"He hasn't got a dime," a third man said. I recognized him as a reporter for the *Cape Codder*, a local paper. "Not a pot to piss in. You know, John feeds him on credit; he can't afford a bottle of beer."

Keep cool, I told myself. After all, some of it was true; the owner of the Land Ho had given me a tab, and I was still overextended. But then the first guy opened his mouth again.

"Clifford's violated the conditions of his permit," he told the others. "I've seen them bringing things on deck." When he turned toward the bartender, I knew who I was dealing with.

Early that summer Billy Crockett had asked if he could work for me. Though he was pleasant enough, I could tell it wouldn't work out. He was used to working for himself, and I didn't think he'd be a team player. After coming to the cape as a teen, he had gotten involved in all sorts of escapades. At one point he was arrested; he claims he was mistaken as a CIA spy off the coast of Cuba. Back home, he started looking for the *Whydah,* even doing some historical research, but whatever hunting he did wasn't very thorough or systematic, and he quit after a few years. Now he painted houses.

I thought we had understood each other, but I had underestimated Crockett's sense of competition.

Walking up between Billy and one of his companions, I told him, "No one is violating the conditions of the permit."

Crockett lost an eye in a car accident; he had to turn all the way around to see me.

"The hell you aren't. You're allowed to inspect the area and identify the wreck. I hate to think what the Archaeology Board would say if they knew what was going on out there."

"What about those coins you said you found? Did they jump into your hand?"

Crockett turned back to his pals. "No they didn't. But you're the one who has the permit." The others laughed along with him.

Most nights I worked late at the Captain's House planning how to make the best use of our diving time and taking care of administrative headaches. That night, after dinner at the Land Ho, I intended to see the kids, but missed the last ferry back to the Vineyard. I told them goodnight over the phone, and then, feeling a little sorry for myself, drove up to the Beachcomber, a bar a few miles north of the site at Cahoon's Hollow where I knew I'd find most of the crew.

You'd have thought working those long hours would have been exhausting, but the crew got so pumped with adrenaline that they'd tie up the *Vast* nearby, swim ashore, change into dry clothes in the men's room, then hit the dance floor. Treasure hunters were great for business—the owners let them in free all season. On the water, we had grown used to onlookers. Occasionally, to get our attention, a free-spirited young woman would take off her top and wave it over her head. That usually worked.

Those women started coming to the Beachcomber, mostly to compete over Kennedy. Beyer had polished his charm shooting photographs for those hotel brochures. He convinced his employers it was a waste of money to fly models to a resort; instead, he scouted the beaches and pools for the most beautiful woman he could find, explain his assignment, then ask if she could do him a favor. The professional model assigned to the shoot was sick; would she fill in?

"I used to think that was a good angle," Beyer told me one night. "But this pirate treasure thing has it beat."

We called him Wile E. Coyote. He'd drive off in his '67 Buick Riviera, nicknamed the Ghetto Jet, with a different girl each night. After three hours of sleep at The Barracks, he'd be up at six, ready to navigate the *Crumpstey* through Nauset Inlet.

Almost everyone who came to the Beachcomber that summer stopped in the parking lot to look at the *Vast*, an odd-looking boat, and they'd eventually ask about "those big metal things." Sometimes we said they were giant underwater periscopes we used for whale-watching; sometimes we said that to finance the treasure hunting we used them to suck up clams. Eventually Scotty posted a sign with possible answers on a flip chart, so they could take their choice.

Watching the crew laughing and shouting, having a good time, I decided against telling them about Billy Crockett. But the little encounter stuck in my craw.

The next morning we went to Captain Elmer's for breakfast. While the others ate eggs, Portugese sausages, and "flippers," pieces of bread fried in olive oil, I told them.

"Crockett was running at the mouth at the Land Ho."

Stretch was already well into his second breakfast. Even in a crowd of men with big appetites, he put down some amazing meals. "You think he wants to cause trouble?"

I shook my head. "You know Billy. His nose is out of joint." The woman sitting alone against the far wall, a spiral-bound notebook open in front of her, seemed to be watching me. "I believe he *wants* to find the *Whydah*. I believe he's *thought about* finding the Whydah."

"Him and the rest of the world," Stretch said.

"Barry. Come over and say hello."

I turned and saw Peter, a friend of mine from Wellfleet; he had just sat down across the table from the woman by the far wall. She was drop-dead gorgeous; Peter was moving up in the world.

After a minute of brainless chatter with him I smiled at his friend and introduced myself.

"I'm Heidi," she said. "Heidi Pearl. From Truro." She had long, light, wavy hair, and an athletic body. "You don't look like tourists. Do you fish?"

Peter laughed.

I told her, "Right now I'm hunting down a pirate ship called the *Whydah.*"

"Oh!" Her voice was soft and lilting, the sort of voice that made you want to lean closer. "I've heard about that."

I wanted to ask her what she had heard—the good or the bad—but instead said, "You're studying?"

"A summer school course at the Community College. Art history."

From across the room, Stretch called, "Barry—you coming?"

Beyer chimed in, "Don't rush yourself. We wouldn't want to interrupt anything important."

"The crew," I told her.

She gave me a five-hundred-watt smile.

I hesitated just a moment, then turned to get back to work.

On the morning of July 28 the board convened a meeting in the National Park Service building near Marconi Station to address some dramatic new business. Suddenly the nine members were all wearing business clothes, their hair slicked back. The crowd of over thirty people included me and Rob and Levin and Allan, Crockett and his friends, a staff member from Senator Doane's office, newspaper reporters, and any number of local gossips.

For a long time the board had virtually no budget—which made sense, seeing as it had nothing to do. They couldn't have realized how their lives were going to be changed by the *Whydah.* It wasn't until that summer, for example—ten years after it was established, and despite the famous feud over the General Arnold—that the board decided someone should be appointed to take minutes of their meetings. In addition to the official secretary, there were now half a dozen men scribbling onto stenographer's pads, including Crockett's friend from the *Cape Codder* who had been at the bar.

After seeing what the currents did to the metal detector and every other loose object, and considering Southack wrote that the *Why-dah*'s wreckage covered four miles back in 1717, I had filed a request for a larger permit area. At the same time, Crockett and a few of his friends had formed something they called Old Blue Fishing Company and requested rights to search the area next to mine.

"We have evidence that we've found the true location of the wreck," Crockett said. "We aren't relying merely on historical documents; we have physical proof." With that his friends hauled out pieces of pottery, nails, and a musketball.

"And where were these items found?" Joseph Sinnott, one of the board members, asked.

"Along the beach adjacent to the permit area we've requested."

"Christ," Rob said. "These guys aren't divers, they're beach-combers."

I snorted. "If that cannonball was sitting on the beach, somebody dropped it from a plane."

In the front of the room, someone on the board asked, "Have you ascertained their age?"

Crockett said, "All of these pieces are over one hundred years old."

"So is half the stuff down there," I told Levin. "What's that prove?"

The board members talked softly among themselves. One of them looked at the ceramic shards, then another picked up the musketball, as if there might be a date on it.

Stalling.

The newspaper reporters held their pens over their steno pads. I held my breath.

"The extension request from Maritime Explorers," Joseph Sin-nott said, "will not be granted until you, Mr. Clifford, can demonstrate that you have found at least part of the wreck of the *Whydah*." Crockett's crew all but shouted; they were on the verge of stealing the treasure out from under me.

"The permit application from the Old Blue Fishing Company," Sinnott continued, "will have to be heard at a public hearing, and not at a regular board meeting such as today's."

"What the hell was that?" I asked Allan when we got out into the sun. "Did I miss something, or did they just go on the record saying they've got no clue what to do?"

"They told you to bring them evidence. Otherwise . . ."

"You think they'd give Crockett a permit?"

"He's done what he's supposed to do, preparing an application and gathering evidence. If they're going to turn him down, they'll need a good reason."

"You know as well as I do," I said, "Crockett is just trying to sabotage us. If the treasure extends beyond our boundary, are you telling me the board is going to give Crockett the rest?"

Allan stopped next to his car. "Two things," he said. "First, the board doesn't understand what you're doing, or what they're doing, and that makes them nervous. They're learning their job as all this happens, and they know this is the biggest project they'll ever be involved with."

"What's the other thing?"

"They don't like you."

Whenever arguments with the board got too loud, or paper pushing with lawyers got too tedious, I practiced a form of meditation. Waking in the morning, I'd concentrate on Southack, trying to see through his eyes. He *knew* where the wreck was; he saw pieces of the ship wash ashore. *Let me find this,* I'd think. *Let me find this . . . and I'll do the right thing.* Whatever that was. Part of the hunt was metaphysical. Then it was on to the physical: getting out of bed, drinking a cup of strong coffee, and heading for the *Crumpstey.*

"The thing that bothers me," I told Brad Crosby as we looked over the charts on the *Vast,* "is we don't know exactly how much the shoreline has receded." Our last pit had turned up more ammunition and an old outboard engine someone had lost.

Brad said, "If your measurements are from points on land, how much difference would it make?"

"Those are too general. If the *Whydah* ran aground, she—"

"Shut it off!" someone shouted. "Shut it down!"

Running from the pilothouse, I saw a strange sight: Todd Murphy was being dragged backward across the deck.

Two of the crew had made a mistake by setting the down-current anchor first; that made the stern anchor line slack, so line began to lay on the deck. Standing in the bow, Todd had turned to the stern to call out to the guys setting the anchors when the *Vast* suddenly moved; a loop of inch-thick line jumped up around his ankle. In the meantime, someone turned on the machine coil to pull the line taut, so Todd was dragged steadily toward the block, where the line fed through a two-inch hole. The machine coil would pull his foot through that hole like meat through a grinder.

"Grab him!" I told Brad. "I'll get his leg." Todd had been dragged to a pulley, where he was sitting up, trying to loosen the line from around his ankle, yelling "Move it forward!" It was one of those moments that seems to last half an hour—Todd yelling, Brad and I trying to free his leg, the line about to snap his foot off. Finally what he was saying sunk in—I issued the command, Stretch moved the *Vast* forward, and the line loosened.

Todd is a Special Forces medic, and he never lost his cool; he slipped the line off his foot and immediately examined his ankle. The line had left a welt the way a rubber band leaves a red circle around your wrist—except the anchor line left a trough in his ankle that you could rest your finger in. The fibers of the rope were burned into his skin.

"It was like watching television," he said later. "All I could think was, 'This really sucks. My foot's coming off. I won't be able to go to Ranger school, won't be able to play sports . . . I'll swim in circles, because one leg'll be shorter than the other."

We got him onto the *Crumpstey*, from there to the clinic on the cape. He wasn't happy with the treatment he got, so he asked for the supplies he needed and went home to take care of himself. He suffered what are called crush injuries: his ankle was deeply bruised, and his whole lower leg turned black. He was through for the season. When he went back to school, he had foot drop—the muscles from the leg to the foot quit working, so when he walked, his foot would just flop on the ground. It didn't heal until well into the winter.

That reminded everyone how important it was to follow procedure, and how quickly an accident could happen. Inexperience was no excuse. A lot of the crew had been in the service, and they knew the importance of maintaining and neatly arranging equipment. Orderliness was essential also because we had so many visitors on both the *Crumpstey* and the *Vast* who didn't know the first thing about boats, so could easily get into trouble. If that wasn't reason enough, we were always being watched by reporters and state officials and people like Crockett looking for ways to stop us. One bad accident and they would say we were careless, or incompetent.

I had one other, slightly more devious reason for insisting on having the boats in top condition: when the weather kept us from diving, which happened frequently, or for some other reason we couldn't be on the water, the crew were more likely to dwell on the fact that they weren't getting much beyond the thrill of the chase in return for their work. They all made jokes about being broke, but I knew some of them missed the security of a weekly paycheck. Working on the boats kept them busy, and it was good for morale.

The best morale booster of the season, though, came the day I found the *Whydah*.

Barry Jr. came into the pilothouse of the *Vast* looking low. Karen, a friend he had brought along that day to see what we were doing, was up on deck.

"My braces hurt."

"Oh yeah?" I looked over the map, thinking. Beyer had just recorded a big hit under the *Crumpstey*—not the very biggest, but when I checked our position against the chart, it felt right.

I felt Barry looking over my shoulder.

"Remember," I told him, "he said they'll probably need adjusting. Are they too tight?"

"They're rubbing against my cheek."

When I looked at him I saw the real problem. The sky had been dark all morning, and now a light rain fell. As the waves had picked up, the *Vast* started into her steady roll. I've never been seasick, so I hadn't realized what was going on. Barry looked green.

"You don't want to be in here," I told him. "Get out in the air. Take deep breaths." Then: "Is Karen sick, too?"

He nodded.

There wasn't anything to do. I just smiled and said he'd be all right.

After getting into position, we anchored the *Vast* over the spot Beyer had identified and blew the pit. I dove without waiting for the water to clear, fanning away the swirling sand, feeling for the bottom. There, running right through the pit—it couldn't have been buried under more than a foot of sand—was what felt like a metal rod. I started digging with my hands; if this was what I thought, it had to be longer. The more I dug, the more certain I was. Crosby came down a minute later, and together we pulled the thing free. After we looped a line around it, the crew used the crane on the *Vast* to haul it up.

Tugging my mask back over my head, I called up to Rob, "Measure that baby!" Before he had found the tape I had jumped up on deck. "Come on, come on."

You never saw a less impressed group of people in your life. The crew looked at me as if I were trying to sell them swampland real estate.

McClung, faithful to the last, took a measure to the rod and said, "Twenty feet, give or take an inch."

"This is it!" I said. "Call Chevrolet! It's time to order those Corvettes."

Bulls-eye. If we had found the mizzenstay, which would have run through the middle of the *Whydah*, we couldn't be far from the treasure.

Someone broke out some beers.

"Hell," Stretch said. "Who would've thought it would be that easy?"

Just then somebody yelled "Wave!"

I looked to the north northeast and saw it rushing from the horizon—a wave fifteen-feet high, coming straight at us.

"Get the divers!" I shouted. "Pull the anchors! Get the *Crumpstey* out of the way!"

Everything happened at once: Rob ran to the mailboxes and started hammering them, our emergency signal to the divers; Bill and Trip ran to the stern to pull the high pressure hoses and anchor lines; the rest of the crew rushed to secure loose equipment; Murphy came up over the side; the *Crumpstey* pulled around to our shore side.

"Get the bow anchor!" I ordered. "Raise the bow anchor!"

Kennedy and Brad bobbed up beside the boat. Brad spit out his mouthpiece.

"What's going on?" he said. "What's the——"

"Get up here!" Rob said, and that voice of his practically propelled Crosby and Kennedy onto the deck.

The wave hit us broadside, crashing over the top of the *Vast*'s pilothouse, swinging us around on the sternline to the southeast. It was an amazing sensation, being under a wave that size, having a boat as big as the *Vast* knocked around like a toy. Not getting that anchor up had saved us. The moment I realized it had held, I looked back to the northeast, prepared for another rogue, but there was nothing out there.

"Bellamy's revenge," Crosby said.

We had been knocked around, but there were no serious injuries. All I could think of was the wave that had capsized one of Mel Fisher's boats, killing his son and daughter-in-law. I looked for Barry.

He stood next to Karen, both of them with eyes like marshmallows.

Stretch told them, "This is the date you'll never forget."

The discovery of the mizzenstay seemed anticlimactic for good reason. Marconi Beach is named after Guglielmo Marconi, the Italian who, at the turn of the century, built an enormous array of steel towers and wires near the cliffs at South Wellfleet to transmit the first transatlantic wireless messages. At the Cape Cod National Seashore Headquarters a few days later I looked at the photos of Marconi's towers and saw they were constructed of dozens of rods just like the one Brad and I had brought up.

We found more of them the rest of that season, and each time the divers would say, "This is it! Call Chevrolet!"

I never thought it was all that funny.

RATS, BATS, AND MUTINY

THE SUN GLINTED OFF THE ocean, blinding, as Jimi Hendrix's "All Along the Watchtower" echoed out across the water from the *Vast*'s speakers. We felt like lizards, scorched by the summer heat, going through what had become our routine. Aboard the *Crumpstey*, Beyer watched the magnetometer readout.

He radioed over to us.

"I think I'm out of our permit area," he said.

Palming the radio mike, Stretch looked over to me.

"What did he say?"

Stretch radioed Beyer, "We can't hear you."

The *Crumpstey* dutifully continued northward.

"Maybe we'll find Dad," said Mike Andrews, our cook.

Back in Bellamy's day a ship's cook was often an older, experienced sailor too ill or worn to do more than give advice and enter a kind of retirement at sea; Mikey, a small Portugese man from Provincetown, was our voice of experience. Years ago, his father had drowned near the *Whydah* site. More than any of us, he had reason to consider the ghosts below us, the spirits of all the men whose ships had wrecked off the cape.

"You never know," I told him. "I feel lucky today."

"Stretch!" Beyer's staticky voice cut through the amplified guitar. "Get over here! The mag is going nuts!"

We jumped into action—which is to say, we got to this new hit, Stretch pointed us into the current, we anchored, adjusted the anchor lines to get us directly over the spot, divers locked the mailboxes into position, and we blew a pit. In a little less than two hours we were ready to dive.

Brad and Stretch climbed into their wet suits, spit into their masks to keep the lenses from clouding, pulled on their tanks, and checked the mouthpieces of their regulators.

They went over the side.

More and more we didn't wait for the sand to settle; the process was slow enough. Stretch fanned the blade of a ping-pong paddle, one of your more high-tech treasure hunting tools, and made out what looked like a stack of crusted bricks. After taking his knife from his leg sheath, he smacked the blocks with the butt end—Bam. Where he hit the blocks, encrustation fell away; what was underneath flashed like a spark.

They came to the surface breathless.

"That's the first time I ever heard anybody yell underwater," Brad said, grinning. "Stretch said, 'Silver!' and then he started grinning like an idiot."

Todd and I suited up. There wasn't much room in the pit; the propwash had exposed what looked like a stack of giant silver ingots. We dug with our hands to fully expose the top of the stack, then got a piece of the stuff on deck. As we knocked off some of the crust, exposing more of the metal, I had to break the bad news.

"Tin."

"Oh man," Stretch said. He didn't have to ask; there was no tin anyone knew of in the cargo of the *Whydah*. "I was sure we had her."

"This is our good luck?" Mikey asked.

"Maybe so," I told him. "You know what? I bet we've found the *White Squall*. She sank in a gale in February 1867, carrying a huge cargo of tin from Malaysia and Indonesia."

Brad said, "What's this stuff worth?"

"About eight dollars a pound," I told him.

"It's worth salvaging," Beyer said. "If it's all right here, it couldn't take that long to bring it up." Then, looking at Brad and Todd: "What's wrong with you guys? If you'd been out here fishing and came across a ship full of tin, you'd think this was the luckiest day of your life."

I said, "Throw out a buoy." While Beyer marked the spot, the rest of us celebrated.

Resting a cold can on the deck rail, Todd asked me, "Have you got every wreck out here memorized? How'd you know about this *Wild Squall?*"

"Hey, Barry," Stretch interrupted. "Look up there, on shore."

I turned toward the Wellfleet cliffs, but saw only a few sunbathers. Shading my eyes to cut the glare, I made out a familiar figure staring back at us. He lowered the binoculars, revealing a black eye patch.

"Now what does that bastard want?"

It seemed we had an audience . . .

A few nights later, the crew moored the *Vast* near the Beachcomber—which happened to be near the *White Squall* site. Stretch stayed aboard to guard our equipment.

It was the heat of the summer; he slept naked in the pilothouse. Long after the music from shore had ended for the night, a loud banging echoed through the boat.

In his usual good humor whenever his sleep was interrupted, Stretch ran out onto the flying bridge, peering into the darkness to find the source of the noise. A skiff had pulled up beside the *Vast*, and by the light of the bow he saw an older man with a sharp nose and one beady eye, the other covered by a patch—the same man who had been watching us from shore. As he banged an oar against the side of the vessel, another man sitting behind him had a shotgun across his lap. It looked like a scene from *Treasure Island*.

"Get the hell off my site," the little man shouted.

Some people might call it courage; others might call it the poor judgment of a man barely awake. Stretch ignored the shotgun.

"If you don't keep that damned oar away from this boat I'll come down there and shove it up your ass."

It must have been quite a sight from that little skiff: Stretch standing up on the bridge, naked, silhouetted against the stars.

"Tell your buddy Clifford he's the biggest liar on the cape."

"Oh yeah? When did you move?"

Matt Costa is a notorious figure on the cape, especially around

Provincetown, his home. People know him because he's a self-made man, a kid from a poor family turned filthy rich. He owns a bar, a restaurant, a motel, and a subdivision. Fishermen hate him because he buys fish dirt cheap. But even more people know Costa as "Rat"—the name comes either from the fact that as a kid he was a wharf rat, or from the way we thought he looked—because of his eye patch. A hunter with a collection of stuffed animals, Costa blew his eye out in a hunting accident.

"You'll go to jail with him!" Costa shouted. "I've got photographs of Clifford digging off his site."

"I'll give you ten seconds to turn around." Stretch towered over the skiff. Then he called out to Costa's pal, "Be careful with that gun, before you blow his other eye out."

I woke up in a sweat.

No light shone through the bedroom curtains. As I reached for the phone, the clock next to the bed read 3:10.

Since it took so long to dig a decent test pit, we were only able to explore a few anomalies a week. While Beyer and I knew the site best, some of the crew were old friends, others were investors; everyone had an opinion. John Levin, in particular, grew increasingly insistent in telling me where he thought we should dig.

Mag readings, historical clues, and financial details spun in my mind like so much prop-wash. During the day I felt more and more distracted, distant from the others. But that night, when I had finally drifted into sleep, all of those things settled, leaving my subconscious mind as clear as the sea in an ad for a tropical resort.

Bellamy appeared. We stood on the deck of another ship, not the *Whydah,* on a calm sea, the sun scorching. In the background I made out the radio broadcast of a Red Sox game; Bellamy shook his head. *The crew,* he said. *I know what you mean,* I told him. We chatted a moment—that is, I sensed that we talked, but I couldn't tell what either of us said—until I worked up the nerve to ask him.

Where is it? I didn't have to name the ship; he knew why I had come.

Bellamy turned away, and for a moment I thought he was about to issue an order to the crew. But he didn't speak. He turned back, but instead of answering he looked right through me. I understood; he couldn't say.

Are we close?

No answer.

Is it within the boundaries of our permit?

Still no words, and no real change in his facial expression, but a hardness came to his eyes that seemed to imply, *Of course.*

What do I have to do? Is there something I'm missing?

This time he spoke; his voice sounded a lot like Fay Feild's.

You thought it was too small, Bellamy told me. *You thought it was too close to shore.*

I knew it! It's the one at—

But then I was bolt upright, dialing.

After two rings Stretch picked up the phone, shouted, "I'll tear your damned head off!" and hung up.

I dialed again.

"Stretch—Barry."

He started to apologize, but I cut him off.

"I know where the *Whydah* is."

"So do I. Underwater."

"I'm serious. I'll call the crew. We're going out."

He grumbled about it being impossible to get any sleep anyway, so why the hell not.

As it turned out, we might as well have gotten a good night's rest. After spending the day at the spot, all we found were more buried drones from long-gone Camp Wellfleet.

"Pretty wild story," Trip said. "I didn't know anybody was still doing LSD."

McClung knew better. "I know what you're going to say," he told me. "Your intuition has gotten us this far. But when it comes to deciding where to dig, I've got more faith in the magnetometer."

"You've got to go with your hunches," Stretch countered, pouring his fifth cup of coffee. "But if that really was Bellamy you heard, he might be trying to throw us off the trail."

.   .   .

Matt Costa ran to the police, who told us we couldn't moor near the *White Squall* site. I was tempted to ask when the Wellfleet Police Department had been given jurisdiction on the high seas, but it seemed wise to keep the law on our side. When I called Bob Cahill, one of the state board members, to stop Costa, I learned Costa had already contacted them himself, claiming we had no right to dive on the *White Squall,* that he and his partners in the Ocean Marine Diving Company had previously located the wreck, and that they had filed for permission to dive on it.

"That's a lot of crap, and you know it," I told Cahill. "Costa has been hanging on like a leech, just waiting to suck us dry."

"I don't know what to tell you," Bob said. "We have to hold a hearing."

After hanging up, I called my answering service to check my messages. Along with a call from Colorado there was one from somebody who said he had a hunting dog we could use, and one from Heidi Pearl.

"There's someone you should meet," the woman at the service read. "She knows everything about local history." She gave me the number.

I jotted it down.

I had transferred my charts from the Vineyard to the Captain's House; now, looking at Southack's map on the wall, I remembered I needed a new pack of pushpins to mark the latest anomolies.

How had she gotten my number?

Well, that was easy enough. And the more I thought about it, Peter hadn't been sitting close to her; they didn't act as if they had planned to meet at Captain Elmer's that morning. But she must have been in her mid-twenties; what could she see in me?

Nothing. She was interested in the *Whydah* and wanted to help.

I picked up the receiver.

The next day Heidi sat in my car, giving me directions to the home of one of her former elementary school teachers.

"So," I said as we drove to this woman's house, "you ever do any diving?"

"Just swimming. And I used to do a lot of running on the beach."

That explained her body. "I'm surprised I never saw you."

"I've been a runner ever since I was little. At Nauset I ran the mile, and the 440. And I did gymnastics. Left here."

I turned, cutting off a tourist's Winnebago.

"So you were a runner and a gymnast."

"And I played baseball."

"Softball?"

"Baseball. I pitched."

"You, what, you tucked your hair under your cap and pretended to be a boy?" Fat chance of that.

"I just pitched. I had a great bean ball."

"Here," Heidi finally said. "Up this little road."

Her elementary school teacher lived in a beautiful, decrepit, rose-covered little house. I thought of Uncle Bill's fishing shack.

The old woman who opened the door had white hair and wore a thin cotton dress. Her red complexion set off tiny blue eyes; if Santa Claus had a mother, here she was. She hugged Heidi as if she were her granddaughter.

"This is Barry," Heidi told her.

"Mr. Clifford," the old woman said, extending her hand. "I've read all about you in the papers."

"I hope you know better than to believe them." She smelled of earth; she had been out in the garden.

Mrs. Holway was amazing. I thought we would talk forever, the three of us as comfortable as old friends. She told us about her garden, then about Truro, giving us names of other people we should talk to if we really wanted to know our history.

"If you don't mind my saying so," Mrs. Holway told me, "you sound like a very confident young man. What makes you so sure you're going to find this ship?"

It had been a while since I had been called a young man. "Some of the pirates were captured, and they confirmed the rumors that the ship had been fully loaded with silver and gold. Most importantly, a representative of the state kept a journal, and that's been very helpful."

Mrs. Holway suddenly looked stern; she gave me a look she must have given hundreds of students. "Mr. Clifford," she said, "I should certainly hope you've done your homework on Cyprian Southack. I taught him to fourth graders for fifty years."

Suddenly I felt a little less smug.

From there Heidi and I went to the site of Samuel Harding's house, where we found the signs of a foundation and pieces of rock and brick. She wanted to hear everything about the *Whydah,* and while we talked I completely escaped bills and lawyers and state regulations. Every voice in my head was telling me to get back to work, get back on the water; but I was like a man caught in a whirlpool.

From Harding's house we went to Cahoon's Hollow beach. It was while we were swimming in Gull Pond that I understood how Sam Bellamy had felt the day he saw Maria Hallett. There was something magical about her—and if I wasn't careful, she might vanish at any moment.

In order to decide who, if anyone, would be awarded a permit for the *White Squall,* the Board of Underwater Archaeological Resources scheduled a hearing for August 25 on the tenth floor of One Winter Street in Boston, the state's office for the Department of Environmental Quality Engineering, at 10:00 A.M. Allan Tufankjian and I opened the conference room door expecting to find the board members shuffling papers, quietly preparing to justify whatever decisions they had reached. Instead, there was pandemonium.

The glare of television lights and flashes of cameras circled me as soon as I entered the room. Beyond the glare, the board members stood in tight circles, dressed like senators.

The room was full of sharks. Costa all but arched his back in preparation for a feeding frenzy when he saw me. Then he turned back to his partners Bill Daniels, a boat salesman who wore polyester suits, and Oscar Snow, a fisherman from an old Pilgrim family. Billy Crockett had teamed up with two other men to stake yet another claim. After watching us chart the site and eliminate anomalies all summer, these guys were trying to grab the *Whydah* for themselves. As Crockett and Costa trained their one good eye on each other, I heard Costa call out across the room, "Bill, you watch that side; I'll take care of this side." I kept my eyes on the board.

The hearing began with hemming and hawing over procedure as

the board members did their best imitations of bad politicians. Things started to get interesting when they proposed an amendment that would allow any person or group to hold only one permit at a time. Allan and I argued against that, and Bob Cahill spoke in our support; still, the majority of the board voted that any person or enterprise could have only one excavation permit. That meant we could only get to the *White Squall,* and so some guaranteed income, if our current permit area was expanded.

The next item on the agenda was to clarify the size of a permit area, which they decided should be one nautical mile square. (The board went about making these decisions as if they could do anything they wanted; in fact, admiralty law covers specifications of site boundaries, and the state of Massachusetts, much less the board, had no right to make up their own rules.)

"We now have before us," Joseph Sinnott declared, "Maritime Explorations' request for extension of the permit area. Mr. Clifford's written request was received over a month ago"—he glanced at his notes—"on July 7, 1983."

"I submit this section of Cyprian Southack's journal, which says that the *Whydah* wreck was dispersed over four miles *at that time,*" I began. "The fact that I've found a cluster of strong anomalies one thousand yards to the north of my permit area substantiates that." I tacked a chart of our magnetometer readings to the front wall to illustrate the scatter beyond our permit area. Reporters and television cameras shuffled closer, though their readers and viewers wouldn't know a mag hit from an infield hit.

"This doesn't exclude the possibility that portions of the *Whydah* also lie to the south of my site," I continued. "You see from this chart that there are anomalies on that side as well. Since we don't know if the storm that wrecked the *Whydah* came from the northeast or southeast, its remains could be on either side. The board has already agreed to salvage this wreck; I'm simply asking that you let me look in adjacent areas, so I can do a complete job."

Allan nodded. He had recommended that we not say anything about the *White Squall,* because admitting that we dove on it meant we had been beyond the boundaries of our permit area. But there was no rule against our diving in open water, and the majority of the board members seemed to be agreeable; I went with the momentum.

"I'm also asking for a second permit," I told them. "In exploring the anomalies north of my border, I found a famous old shipwreck called the *White Squall.*" I passed them some photographs of iron straps and other artifacts we had found the day we discovered the tin. They huddled over the pictures, passing them along.

Valerie Talmage, one of the board's state archaeologists, was unimpressed. "As to your first request, Mr. Clifford," she said starchily, "most experts agree that flotable debris from shipwrecks is widely scattered, but that the central, heavy portion of a ship remains localized. Further, identification of such a wreck is difficult; even the presence of an early eighteenth-century artifact assemblage would not be persuasive. We need more information on other wrecks in the area, the context of what has been excavated so far, and more historical research regarding specific artifacts."

Talmage's attitude was going to reappear in various guises; like a lot of academic archaeologists, she thought treasure hunters should be shoved back into the holes they crawled out of. On top of that, she didn't know anything about the day-to-day work of underwater excavation—and she knew I knew it.

Billy Crockett's group, the Old Blue Fishing Company, stepped up to ask for a permit south of my site. Even here Billy was casual and rumpled, as if he had just stepped off his boat. As proof that they'd found something, one of his partners held up a cannonball they claimed came from the *Whydah.*

"This is crazy," I whispered, not so softly, to Allan. "Anybody in this room can *buy* one of those."

Allan shrugged.

"Where's their documentation?" I said, standing.

The board refused to recognize me; they asked Crockett for some clarification, then complimented him on the thoroughness of Old Blue's application. Charles Sanderson, who still came to each meeting to report on his hopeless search for the *General Arnold,* shot me a look so smug I wanted to deck him.

Then Costa, Snow, and Daniels stood, going for the knockout. They requested a permit for the area to the north of mine, where we'd found the *White Squall*. They had photographs of artifacts—a coin, an anchor, a ship's rib, a button—claimed to have been found on the site forty years ago. If everyone who had ever found a coin could claim rights to the site, divers were going to have to stand in line. And if these guys were so anxious to start treasure hunting, why had they spent the whole season on land?

"Wait a minute," I whispered to Allan, loud enough for the board to hear. "Did Snow just say *scuba diving?*"

Allan nodded.

"Cousteau had barely *invented* scuba forty years ago."

Allan made a note; the board called for a short break.

Costa, Crockett, and I each mapped our requested permit areas on a chart in the front of the room. We didn't talk. When we stepped back, the board moved in. After a hushed discussion, they reconvened.

The board had a tough call to make; no matter what they decided, a lot of people were going to be angry. So after spending the beginning of the hearing exercising authority that wasn't legally theirs and changing regulations to suit themselves, now they decided to fall back on the old rules, which said that all applications would be considered in the order received. One member said my application for the *White Squall* was incomplete, so shouldn't be considered at all.

"That's ridiculous," I said, not even pretending to whisper. "This is a disaster."

They didn't listen. When the votes were taken, Old Blue and Ocean marine got what they'd asked for. The board went on to create a 0.4 nautical mile buffer zone around each permit area, which was absolutely useless. They thought a line on a map would keep Costa off our territory. We were going to have to protect ourselves. Somewhere, Bellamy's ghost was enjoying this.

"The state law that created this body," Allan said, standing, "was intended to govern the excavation of shipwrecks, not simply the exploration of a permit area. This decision would appear to be in direct contradiction of the intent of that law."

The board members huffed and puffed; Talmage responded by

warning me from digging any more pits outside of my permit area, missing the point completely.

The meeting finally ended at 3:40, five hours after it had been officially convened.

Crockett told a television reporter, "My partners and I think we've located the wreck, and from what the board just decided it looks like they agree."

Costa was huddled with a Boston newspaperman, no doubt calling me a liar and spreading his own brand of "truth."

"I don't know who I want to hit first." Allan and I stepped into the elevator. "All the board cares about anymore is how they'll look on television. As long as everyone follows their procedure, they couldn't care less about 'cultural resources.' "

Allan didn't answer. Then I noticed that the other two passengers riding with us were newspaper reporters, scribbling away.

"Print it," I told them. "Write the truth for a change."

The doors opened onto the lobby. When the reporters were out of earshot, Allan finally spoke. "No one has tested the board's authority."

That's what I wanted to hear.

"Sue," I told him. At least they'd know we meant business.

On the last Sunday of August a flock of coot flew overhead; for me that's always been the first sign of autumn. The day started gray, the sky filled with that diffuse light amateur painters on the cape are always trying to capture. In late morning the rain came, soft and steady. Leaves had a hint of red to them, and the breeze carried the pungent smell of decaying underbrush.

A year earlier I had escaped domesticity by pursuing the *Whydah;* now I escaped the complications of a large-scale treasure hunt with Heidi. When weather kept us from working the next few days, she and I were inseparable. In good and bad moods, Birgitta was quiet; she would be calmly supportive or she could turn cold with anger. For months she had shown the sort of polite interest in the *Whydah* that represented, for her, true anger.

Heidi was not only young but wildly passionate, and I got caught up in something I hadn't felt since the early months with Patsy during college. We ran in the woods together, swam, and spent long hours talking; it was as if we had been separated for years and had to catch up.

The skies cleared, but soon we had new problems. Rob had to fly back to Colorado for a week, Stretch picked up a bad ear infection, and through a minor brush against some old metal Brad Crosby wound up with a leg infection that forced him into the hospital. Todd and Trip and I worked on the *Vast*, hoping to find something before the season shut us out.

One day in early September, Beyer recorded a huge hit close to shore; whatever was down there, there was a lot of it. McClung had returned by that time, and he dove the pit first. Visibility was terrible—the mung weed had started to rot, and it blew all around us. Rob reached out and felt the sandy walls of the pit, digging lightly, and found nothing but more sand. Using his fins, he propelled himself slowly to the top of the pit—and it's a good thing, because if he had gone up much faster he probably would have knocked himself unconscious. He burst to the surface shouting.

"It's a hull!" he said. "I got caught under it."

"Is it exposed? What could you see?"

"It's wooden—and it's upside down."

Beyer and Murphy went down and saw huge, heavy timbers. That day I spent six hours underwater. The wreck was double strapped with iron, and from the looks of the edge of the hull, it appeared to be large.

I never slept well, but that night I was even more restless than usual. The press was always asking if we had found anything, and that evening I told them this might be it. I thought about that, and the idea of touching the ship Bellamy had walked on—but then I thought of the precautions we needed to take in uncovering and eventually removing the hull, making sure it wasn't damaged, not disturbing the area around it any more than necessary before we knew what else was there.

The next day we dug holes along the direction of the main wreckage, exposing timbers one hundred feet long, along with some nails and what looked like a human rib bone.

The excitement rallied the troops; everybody worked hard, reporters made trips out on the *Crumpstey*, crowds watched from the beach. Rob demonstrated a real talent for drawing; he constantly made sketches of what he saw underwater, the artifacts we raised, and the *Whydah* as he imagined it. John Beyer, who had a case of treasure fever so serious he had been doing mag surveys on the crew's days off, couldn't be pried away from the *Crumpstey*.

"So how does it feel?" a reporter asked me the third day we dove the wreck. "Here you are in the bottom of the ninth and you hit the home run. What do you think people would have said if you had had to pack up for the season without finding it?"

"Those are two different questions," I told him, "and they're both premature. We can't be certain yet what we've found."

"All summer he's Mr. Optimist," Rob said, still in his wet suit, dripping. "Then we finally find it and he acts like this. It's just because I found it, you know. I was the first one down there."

The rest of the crew was the same way; they were angry when I told them the wreck didn't feel right. It didn't fit the evidence. And what I couldn't tell anyone was that if Maria had been the reason Bellamy hugged the cape too closely, the parallel in my own life was obvious: Heidi was dangerous. I wasn't getting much sleep, I doubted some of my judgements. I was in trouble. And as proud as I felt that Jenny, Barry Jr., and Brandon wanted to be on board when we identified the *Whydah*, it was a bad moment when I saw Birgitta had come, too.

"What good was your intuition last time?" John Levin said. "You've got to stop playing your hunches and start using your eyes."

So I didn't explain—but I wasn't surprised when some experts looked over the metal strapping we had raised and told us it was too recent to have been from the *Whydah*. Birgitta tightened her lips, but didn't say a word.

Our next big hit led us to the steel hull of the *Castegna*, which had sunk in 1914.

"Any treasure?" Todd asked. After the *White Squall*, the others knew we had to get the most out of our permit area.

"Of a sort," I said. "The *Castegna* was loaded with guano. Bat shit."

"What do you think, John," Mikey asked Beyer at lunch. "Come up with any marketing schemes? Maybe a New York specialty store?"

"We could give it to Costa," someone said, "but he's already full of it."

Beyer hadn't joined in; he looked serious. "We've been chasing megagammas all summer, and we've found nothing but recent stuff. Maybe next year we should concentrate on smaller hits."

"*Next* year?" one of the divers said.

Conversation stopped.

"This is just the beginning," I said. "We still haven't charted half the permit area."

No one answered. I understood that if I asked for a vote of confidence, I was sunk.

After lunch, Stretch came up by my side. "Barry, while you've been in seventh heaven with Heidi Pearl, the crew has been getting mutinous."

That was the night my room in the Captain's House started to spin.

FIRST STRIKE

"THIS ISN'T THE END OF the world," said Eugene Brunelle, one of our divers. "Did anybody really think we were going to come out here for the summer, scoop up a few million dollars worth of gold, and go shopping for Jaguars?"

A bunch of us were sitting around the Captain's House drinking tea and coffee. The weather had kept us from diving for the past two weeks, and the boats were in top condition; there wasn't much for the crew to do.

"This is a big operation," Stretch agreed. "If people have been trying to find this ship for almost three hundred years, you can't expect it to fall into your lap."

But that wasn't Brunelle's point. "I've been talking to some friends of mine about this wreck off Nova Scotia. The *Feversham*." Eerily thin, Eugene had mushroom-white skin and spoke with an odd hillbilly accent. "It's loaded with treasure. Southack mapped where it went down six years before the *Whydah*."

Levin said, "You think it would be easier to find it than this thing out here?"

"Are you kidding? Anything would—"

"Shut up," I told Brunelle. "If you want to jump ship, just do it. I don't need any quitters hanging around." I also didn't need mutineers. Everyone on the crew had to be bent on a common goal: the *Whydah*.

Levin turned on me. "Speaking of hanging around, Captain, maybe if you weren't spending all your time with that mermaid of yours we'd have made some progress by now."

"Keep Heidi out of this," I said stonily. But when I looked for support, I saw that she had everything to do with the tension among the crew. She had wanted to come out on the boat, so for the past month she had sunbathed on deck, diving in for a swim when the sun grew too hot. A wonderful cook, she had moved into the Captain's House.

"This is Barry's baby," Stretch told Levin. "Nobody's committed to it like he is."

"Look who the hell's talking," Todd added. "You sleep until noon, you've got friends staying here all the time, and when you finally get within sight of the boats you say, 'What's that dirt doing there? Why isn't there more ice?' "

"It's not my job," Levin began, flushing, "to hold your hand on the water. I'm not the one——"

"Just what the hell *is* your job?" Trip said. "Besides charging all your meals to the company, what exactly do you do?"

"I'll tell you what I'm *not*." Levin's eyes were like bullets. "I'm not the captain. I'm not a diver. And I'm not the director of operations. I'm the business manager."

A shot below the belt. Rob had printed his own business cards proclaiming himself director of operations, though no one had officially given him that title. The day he heard about them, Levin gave me a look that said, *I was right about him.*

A lot of the crew didn't always get along with Rob. He didn't spend anywhere near as much time on the water as they did, and to them he was wasting a lot of time.

"You know," someone said as the shouting died down, "Eugene's right about one thing. We gave it a shot, and we haven't found a single piece of hard evidence, real evidence, that the *Whydah*'s there. I know about the research, I know it *should* be there . . ."

"It's there," I said. "Anybody who doesn't want to be here to see it can get out."

Todd looked over in silent support.

"Well," Eugene said, standing, "I've got to run some errands."

A few days later he was gone.

. . .

"I understand," I said into the phone one afternoon. Then: "Yeah, I know what you mean." Then: "I know it. You're right."

When I hung up, Rob said, "Who's leaving now?"

After Labor Day, the crew started finding winter jobs, drifting away. Some of them had survived the summer by making the rounds of the grocery stores on Sunday, eating samples of cheese-flavored crackers and all-beef franks. By Halloween, Stretch was so strapped for cash that he drew his son a picture of a pumpkin.

So I understood. All the same, it felt like desertion.

Now I was looking at a long winter off the water. Even Heidi took off temporarily, leaving me in the Captain's House with Levin and Rob—not exactly the ideal roommates. McClung constantly needled Levin, and John responded by telling me, more than once, "One of us has to go—him or me." But Levin was one of my major investors; Rob was my best friend.

Yankee magazine published an article with the painfully accurate title, "Not the Best Times for Barry Clifford." Like so many reporters, that one had acted like a friend while he was trying to get a story, then he wrote a piece filled with all the gossip and talk of dissension he could dig up. In the summer I hadn't bothered responding to critics, knowing we could prove them wrong by finding the *Whydah* before the week was out. Now I couldn't do anything but take the punches.

If that wasn't bad enough, I had developed one of the worst kinds of physical trouble a diver can get. I had lost most of the hearing in my left ear from diving too much; as soon as I lay down at night, the room began violently spinning. I woke up on a pillow damp from the draining water. So even when I managed to shut out the rest of my nightmares, I spent the off-season wondering whether I'd ever be able to dive again.

When I thought things couldn't get worse, the board wrote to tell me that, because we didn't have a qualified archaeologist, they were revoking my excavation permit for noncompliance. I told them I had tried to get an archaeologist, but almost anyone with the credentials they wanted would have nothing to do with a private salvage operation. As far as I could see, archaeologists were just another bunch of back-stabbing academics waging petty wars. Until I found one who would work with us, I was dead in the water.

"Look at the bright side," Allan told me. "Winter's almost here. You couldn't do any digging if you wanted to."

If Heidi hadn't come back when she did, I would have been living alone. In November I rummaged around the house for my tape recorder, meaning to dictate another plea for money. I found it in McClung's room. No big deal. I rewound the tape, then hit Play, just to make sure I wouldn't record over anything important.

"Barry's gone crazy," Rob's voice said. "He can't find the treasure, and now he's running around with this girl half his age." A long pause. Then: "I've got to get out of here."

After all I had done for Rob, defending him to the crew, saving his job—after all that, he was going to abandon ship.

A few days later he actually told me, face to face. And Rob had another surprise.

"Levin and I are starting a film production company in Malibu."

"You two are talking to each other?"

"We get along all right."

"Since when do you know anything about movies?"

"I know the right people," he said. "The company's called III MAR, for Rob Alexander McClung, backwards."

He was out of his mind. That was the only answer.

He kept going. "We're going in with Michael Herstadt."

"What the hell are you doing getting mixed up with him?" Herstadt was an Aspen multimillionaire with an unsavory reputation. Like Levin, he liked to be seen with Rob, but he was only going to take advantage of him.

"He's got the cash," Rob said, "and I know a hot starlet when I see one." He grew serious. "Look, Barry, there's nothing here for me. Maybe not for you, either. I'm sorry this *Whydah* thing didn't work out."

Whydah thing?

I thanked him, mumbling something like "Good luck." But when I hung up, I felt like the last rat on a sinking ship.

◆ ◆ ◆

In winter on the cape the east wind blows off the ocean, and the sun rarely struggles through the clouds. The days are short and gray, and only the hard-core residents see the season through. Stretch and Beyer and I braved the weather to record a few last mag surveys before packing it in.

One afternoon I broke the frost off the mailbox, yanked the door open and found one of those make-your-own postcards postmarked from Malibu. One side showed Rob wearing a shoulder-length black wig, standing next to Herstadt's Ferrari, his arm around a buxom Hollywood hopeful. The whole thing looked like a parody of some poor guy's mid-life crisis. On the back McClung had written, "III MAR's going great guns."

I got the message.

The next week I went out to the *Vast* only to find it covered with birdshit. I felt like taking a photograph and making my own postcard.

Birgitta and I talked about what would happen if we split up; she didn't know Heidi, but it was obvious whatever we had shared on the Vineyard was over. Living on the cape, I didn't see the kids enough. I called them, but with every call they sounded more distant. I felt a range of emotions that winter, all of them intensely: love, guilt, determination, loss. There wasn't much snow, but that just served to make the cold seem that much more bleak.

Heidi and I kept a fire going to save on the heating bill. Bundled up against the raw winds, we took walks past the site of Jeremiah's Gutter, past Nauset Inlet, to the deserted beaches. The world was against us. She got a job at a health food store a few days a week, and with what she earned and what little I had left she bought the ingredients for what she called "survival dinners," which always included wonderful breads and cakes.

One miserable day I sat poring over what must have looked to Heidi like just some junk mail. She danced idly around the kitchen, waiting for dinner to be ready, stopping just long enough to look over my shoulder. "Okay," she said, "I'll bite. What's a Motorola Mini-Ranger?"

"Do you really want to know?"

"Give me the short version."

"The magnetometer and Loran obviously aren't telling us everything we need. Loran is only accurate within fifty to one hundred feet—which is okay when you're trying to navigate the ocean, but is the equivalent of you telling one of your customers she can find tofu 'in the back.' " What really worried me was the possibility that we had passed over the cannons without knowing it.

Heidi said, "So this is instead of Loran?"

"The Mini-Ranger is accurate to within a meter. Not only that but it gives you an almost instantaneous readout." We could program a specific survey path, or series of lines for the boat to follow, and be sure of covering the site thoroughly. The Mini-Ranger also allowed us to review our course and the mag readings on a video display, which sure beat pouring over miles of strip chart.

"So how much is it?"

"Too much," I told her.

She opened the oven door to check on dinner. "We could hold a bake sale."

I dropped the mail back on the table. "Why don't I ever think of these things?"

Understand this: I never thought of giving up.

The *Whydah* treasure was still there, the same place it had been at the beginning of the summer, the same place it had been when I sat on the nets in Uncle Bill's fishing shack, more or less where it had been when Southack rowed out in that April storm to claim it for the governor.

We had gone through the initial $250,000 and much more in credit. Lazier and Salloway, out in Colorado, sent some additional money, but because of the way our company was structured they couldn't go back to the original investors. Salloway put me in touch with a Minnesota lawyer named Bucky Zimmerman who was interested in what we were doing and thought he could raise a million dollars through another private offering. By then I could recognize the sort of man who can make a deal work; when I got back from a meeting in Minneapolis I felt confident again that I wasn't going to grow old telling stories about the treasure that got away.

I lined up a local man with an archaeological background to solve our permit problem with the board. At the same time, Todd Murphy convinced Viking America to let us use six dry suits as a promotion. Wet suits allow a thin film of water next to your skin; your body heats the water, which in turns slows down your cooling. Dry suits keep water out altogether, so they're much warmer. They're made of heavy, vulcanized rubber with a neckseal, hood, and feet attached. Underneath, you wear a bunny suit, a sort of foam underwear.

Murphy must have done some fast talking; he also got Viking America to loan us some state-of-the-art equipment made by a company called Aga. Aga tanks are highly pressurized, therefore smaller and easier to carry on your back. Aga masks cover your entire face and include the regulator; breathing in requires less effort, and if we could ever afford to buy a communications system, we'd be able to talk.

Considering I didn't have any money, and our credit was less than sterling, I didn't plan any other purchases. But when the board approved our permit again—still pinning me between Costa and Crockett—they ordered us to conduct "remote sensing surveys" to map what was under the sand before we used the mailboxes. They were afraid the prop wash would damage the artifacts we hadn't found yet. That meant finding someone with side-scan sonar and a sub-bottom profiler, very sophisticated and very expensive equipment.

Just as Heidi and I started to eat, the phone rang. "Is Barry Clifford there?"

"Speaking."

The guy identified himself as a local reporter. The press hadn't stopped just because diving season had ended. The cape has more newspapers than there is news to fill them. I suspected there was at least one shark behind this latest round of attacks.

"I've heard a rumor," this guy said. "People are saying you're going to plant fake artifacts on the site in order to verify your claim."

I took the old advice, but I only counted to five.

"I hadn't thought of that," I told him. "Do you think it would work?" Then I hung up.

How can you manufacture coins encrusted with hundreds of years of oxidation? Where was I going to rent eighteenth-century cannons? I would have ignored those reporters, but there was always the chance the board would take them seriously and give away my permit.

"That's the whole point," Heidi said. "They're trying to wear you down."

Late in the winter I got an even more bizarre phone call.

"Hey, Barry—how's things?"

There are some voices you'll recognize as long as you live.

I asked McClung, "So how's life in the fast lane?"

"You haven't heard? The film company's blown to hell. Herstadt got murdered."

"The movie business must be more dangerous than I thought."

"Levin went to Nova Scotia with Brunelle," Rob said. "They're going after the *Feversham*."

"Two black spots."

In *Treasure Island*, the pirates give a piece of paper bearing a large black circle to shipmates who have gone wrong—it meant they were going to be killed. When I broke all ties with someone, never wanted to see or hear them again, I mentally gave them the black spot.

"So I guess I'll be back," Rob said.

"On a sinking ship?"

"Yeah, well." That was the beginning and end of the apology. We knew each other too well. He added, "We'll see if we can't pump her out."

When we had those first morning meetings on the front lawn of the Captain's House in 1983, my confidence and enthusiasm galvanized the others. In late spring of 1984, I was still confident in my original research, and looked for our new equipment to prove Southack right.

Now my concerns were money and the crew. Some, like Brunelle, left for good; others, like Kennedy and Brad Crosby, wanted to come back but had other obligations. One or two came back for the wrong reasons; to escape other obligations or maybe even for the women at the Beachcomber. But as spring came to the cape and boats returned to the water, the core of the old crew found that, despite all the perfectly understandable reasons not to spend another summer working hard but coming up empty handed, they were victims of treasure fever once again.

Best to get the bad news out of the way. "I don't know what to tell you about getting paid," I began that first morning. "I'll give you what I can, when I can—"

Someone asked, "We get paid?"

The others laughed. The speech I had prepared wasn't important to the faithful; it was for the ones who had cut out.

"This is better," Stretch said. "We don't need all that deadweight on board."

"Divers dive," Todd added. "Scum floats." Todd's dedication was never a question; he was living in his Toyota in the parking lot at the harbor.

As I described the new equipment, I could tell they were eager to give it a try. Nobody expected to have pockets full of gold by the end of the week; they knew we had plenty of work ahead of us. "As long as we use this technology correctly," I told them, "as long as we follow every programmed line the Mini-Ranger dictates, and we plug all the right information into the computer, sooner or later we'll have the treasure."

For the first run of the season through Nauset Inlet, we loaded the *Crumpstey* with six scuba tanks, the magnetometer, bags of supplies, and a reporter. The hull slapped the waves hard; the crew, including Barry Jr., chatted over the roar of the engine while the poor reporter bounced like a tennis ball. He dove for his pencil, but it lurched over the side.

"There are three sandbars in this inlet that could kill us," Charlie Burnham told him.

"You're speaking figuratively, of course." Heavy spray arced over the gunwale; his notebook got soaked.

Charlie thought it over. "Actually, only the third one could really kill us. The first two would just wreck the boat." Then: "You're a good swimmer?"

Before the reporter could answer, we reached the sandbar, the *Crumpstey* rose, and everybody got shaken good.

"We had less than ten inches of water there."

"A foot, easy," Beyer said. "My mother could've gotten us through."

After his first dive, Rob climbed aboard the *Vast* wearing the look of the victim of a practical joke. "You must have had some big-time storms while I was gone."

I keep a log, and every morning I note the weather. Storms don't slip by. "Not particularly."

"We're working with a clean slate," he said.

The contour of the ocean bottom had been dramatically rearranged since fall. Enormous amounts of sand had been displaced; it was like land around a volcano after an eruption.

Logic said we should start at one end of our site and gradually move across it; logic said we should check out every good-sized accumulation of metal. But using the Mini-Ranger meant setting up two towers on the beach, roughly two miles apart, each morning, and collecting them every evening, in the meantime hoping no one would disturb them. After a few weeks it became clear that the logical plan would consume the entire season, if not longer, and research and instinct told me the treasure was much more likely to be in some areas than others. At night I looked back at Southack's journal, hoping that just maybe, after all our work, some offhanded comment would take on new meaning. While there were no surprises, one night I kept stopping at a detail I didn't know how to use.

"Head south," I told Beyer the next morning. "Look back there. Southack said she went down by the tableland." Tableland was, simply, a long flat stretch of shore.

"There's been a lot of wind through here since then."

"And the shoreline has eroded. But I'm guessing the tableland has only moved inland, not shifted north or south." I threw a marker buoy over the side, totally ignoring the mag readings and the Mini Ranger program.

"What's he doing?" Beyer asked Murphy.

Todd shrugged. "He's the captain."

That spot didn't pan out, but from time to time I'd try. The crew called it "psycho magging," and I heard about it when one of my hunches turned up another rod from that damned Marconi tower. Still, we had all spent enough time on the water to believe in mysterious forces.

By mid-summer we built up an enormous, worthless collection of dummy bombs and spent shells from Camp Wellfleet, and the Marconi rods sent the mag sensor flying. But we kept doing the logical thing.

The first glimmer of sunlight easing over the horizon on July 19 found me in Wellfleet, looking over the cliffs Thomas Davis had climbed, trying to find a good spot for an interview. A camera crew from Boston's NBC affiliate wanted to film an update on our search for a weekend news feature. The reporter, Nancy Fernandez, had been talking to me for weeks about doing a story, and she was impatient. I kept putting her off; another major story about us coming up empty handed would only discourage investors, set Costa and Crockett to gloating, give the board more reason to try to shut us down, and generally spoil my naturally sunny disposition.

Describing Maria's wait for Bellamy, and Davis and Julian's escape from the storm over the same ground I stood on, would entertain the station's viewers—and, with any luck, keep Fernandez off the *Vast*. It had gotten to the point that we couldn't afford to waste the gas to shuttle her and her crew to the boat and back. Besides, I didn't need to see news footage of McClung and Murphy hauling up handfuls of .50 caliber machine gun shells. (Headline: *Clifford Bombs Out.*)

I met the crew at The Barracks and together we drove to breakfast. Mornings at Captain Elmer's were a memory from our high-rolling days; that summer we dined at the Stop and Shop.

"Hey, John, hold on." Bill Dibble picked through the coins from his pocket. "I'll split a quart of milk with you."

"It's a good thing they give free refills on coffee," Todd said, holding two donuts and a styrofoam cup. "Too bad they don't make it thicker."

I had just written my last good check for fuel for the boats. When the tanks ran dry, I didn't know what we would do.

The girl at the cash register, a high school kid making spending money, smiled. "You're the treasure hunters, right?"

"That's us," Scotty Magoun said. Scotty was always eager to be recognized as one of the crew; compared to the rest, he was still a kid.

I looked through my wallet; four ones.

"So," she said, "have you found it yet?"

Murphy snorted. "Yeah. Before we could only afford the miniature donuts."

"I must be out of my mind," Dibble said. "I'd be making more money singing on some streetcorner."

"Thanks," I told the cashier, gathering up the donuts. "Keep the change."

"You look like you need it," she said, handing me a shiny penny. "For luck."

The sky was overcast—not black, but a discouraging gray. The gloom covering the ocean seemed like it might stay around for days.

Beyer, Stretch, and McClung went out to the *Vast,* frantically retargetting locations where we'd gotten big hits before. Rob tried to convince me that showing the television camera junk iron would be better than showing it nothing; on television, if there's no picture, there's no story. I resisted, but my ploy never had a chance.

"What do you mean?" Nancy Fernandez said. "We have to go out on the water. This is a water piece."

I tried to explain that our day-to-day operation wasn't very exciting. "We look like a bunch of fishermen," I told her.

One of the camera crew shook his head. "In this light we're sticking to close-ups. We need a picture of the skull and crossbones, and you guys in your Whydah T-shirts. Maybe some guys diving, and dropping those metal things over the propellers."

"Well, let's get some background," I said. "I'll tell you a little about the wreck." I took them out on the *Crumpstey,* going near our site but farther out to sea, describing the *Whydah* and the storm that had beaten Bellamy. "It might've looked something like the storm that's coming in right now," I told Fernandez.

The weather had grown increasingly forbidding. Clouds lurking to the southwest moved up the coast. A chilly, damp wind was blowing offshore. It felt more like April than July.

The cameramen flipped a switch, then lowered the camera from his shoulder. "This is nothing," he said to himself, but loud enough for me to hear. "They're never going to run this."

"Barry, that's a great story about the pirate and Maria Hallett and the crew and the wreck," Nancy said tactfully. "But we ran it last summer."

"Hey!" I raced the *Crumpstey* to the northeast, away from the *Vast.* "Over there! Did you see that whale?"

The crew was still magging when we got there. The cameraman had been enthusiastic about the prospect of whale footage, and I drove fast enough to take their minds off the *Whydah*, but the fuel gauge indicator kept dropping. Besides, we never saw a whale.

Once we boarded the *Vast*, the cameraman immediately began elaborate experiments in an attempt to take a shot of the underwater video monitor we had added since last season. "It will let everybody see what you see when you're down there," Nancy told Rob.

Rob said, "On a good day, we see sand."

Meanwhile, we kept magging. Television crew or no, it looked as if the weather was going to shut us out, and we wanted to get some work done. Beyer reminded me of a spot about a mile south of the Marconi tower and fifteen hundred feet from shore; there weren't any big hits there, but we had mapped some small ones. I always remembered it as the spot I had first marked with an X on my map in 1982; I had been disappointed when the mag's needle hadn't jumped off the chart.

"At least we know something's there," Stretch said. "There might be something worth showing on television."

It was three o'clock; the clouds had grown heavier. I ordered Stretch to anchor over the anomoly cluster. With the surf kicking up, anchoring and blowing the test pit was tricky work; at least, I thought, we looked squared away.

"Barry." Rob planted a hand on my shoulder. "I'll dive this one, all right?"

He didn't know what he wanted more; to talk to Nancy or show up as the diver on the video monitor, like something out of one of those public television specials.

I told Stretch to go down with him. It was frustrating having to stay out of the water, but my ear still gave me trouble.

About ten minutes after they went down, McClung surfaced and didn't bother taking his mask off for the camera. "There's something sticking out the side of the pit."

"How exciting!" Nancy said.

Stretch came to the surface, letting his regulator drop from his mouth. "You getting this on tape?"

"Seriously," I said, leaning over the side, "what'd you find?"

"I don't know," Stretch said. "But they aren't shells, and they're too big around to be part of the Marconi towers."

"There's some big piece of iron," Rob said, "and it's not a fucking Buick, I'll tell you that."

With that he and Stretch slid their masks down, put in their regulators, and went back under.

"Wasted," the television crew's producer said glumly. "We've got to get him to do that Buick line without the f-word."

As we waited, lightning flashed; thunder rolled across the sky. Visibility underwater was too poor for the monitor to show much of anything, and we had all been through enough false alarms to know better than to get enthusiastic about what could be just another piece of junk.

But then they broke the surface together, smiles wider than their face masks.

Rob said, "We're tied off on a cannon!"

You would've thought the deck had turned into a trampoline. That fast, we were all in the water.

About thirty-five feet down, sand floated thickly. Fanning it away, I saw three cannon muzzles, heavily encrusted with concretions, protruding from the sides of the pit. Beside them were some grapefruit-sized chunks.

I'd like to tell you that I spent a moment hovering above the spot, watching the others carefully moving sand away from the cannon, thinking about the agony Bellamy's men had gone through 267 years earlier at the end of the most terrifying night of their lives, their final night, as their ship turned over and these cannons ripped through the decks. But that was their story.

This was mine.

We all took turns clearing away sand, exposing still more concretions—it was impossible to tell what they hid. I lifted one of the grapefruit-shaped objects and took it to the camera crew waiting on deck.

Over the *Vast*, the sky had turned purplish-black. Nancy and the crew gathered around as I slipped off my tank and weight belt. Kneeling, I pried at the object with my knife; the accumulated crust began to fall away.

"A cannonball," I said aloud as the crew drew closer. But there was something else, I could feel it under there . . .

Lightning flickered again.

"Rain," Stretch said, warning the others to begin stowing equipment.

No one moved.

"It looks like a shell," the cameraman said.

"Shell my ass."

"Barry," Nancy said. "If you could watch your language . . ."

"Holy shit," I said. The concretion fell away, exposing a blackened silver coin. "This is a piece of eight."

I kept rubbing, making out a Spanish cross, then a date: 1684.

The crew shouted, laughed, all the things you'd expect; but what I remember is the sky going black above the white cliffs of Wellfleet; the theme from "Ghostbusters" playing on the *Vast*'s radio; and the rain suddenly hammering down. Bellamy is a hard man to ignore.

Someone yelled, "Let's get out of here," and with that we hauled in our lines.

The presence of the television crew kept us from celebrating as wildly as we might have; when Stretch took the *Vast* up to Provincetown, a few of the others went with him just to be able to let their hair down.

When we got the *Crumpstey* back to the inlet, I found even more reason to believe in hunches and instinct.

Heidi was waiting for me, which wasn't so surprising, but she was done up, her hair flowing back around her shoulders in the breeze, wearing her favorite light cotton dress and holding her shoes in her hands. She looked beautiful. She was smiling as if she knew I'd found it—after I told her, she said she had had a premonition something special was going to happen.

The *Whydah* ghosts worked in mysterious ways.

By the time we got back to shore, the banks were closed, so I stashed the things we had brought up—the coin and a few other mysterious concretions—in a foot-high, two-foot-long plastic box filled with salt water to protect them from the air. After searching for a good hiding place, I finally just pushed the box into a dark corner of the basement of the Captain's House. The garage had been filled with concretions for the past year, and no one had ever bothered them. On second thought, I took off the lid and put the coin in my pocket.

As soon as they heard what had happened, the people at the Land Ho made room for our celebration party; it included us, our friends and families, and every reporter we had ever seen, including a crew from the *Today* show.

People who wouldn't talk to me over the winter said they had been rooting for me all along. Still, I couldn't lose myself in the celebration. I kept wanting to say, "Listen—we only have *one coin*."

Beyer told a reporter, "I know this sounds nuts, and I don't believe in reincarnation, but since last summer I've had the feeling we've done all this before. I mean, I didn't know a magnetometer from a toothbrush, but after I got out there . . . there was never any question. Not for me."

Much later that night, I brought the box of treasure from the cellar, refilled it with water—the plastic had cracked—and stowed it under my bed. Heidi's breathing turned slow and regular, but I couldn't sleep. I stared up at the ceiling, Heidi on one side, a rifle on the other. Word had spread all over the cape, all over Boston; I didn't really expect Costa and Crockett to break into my house, but hundreds of people knew where we lived.

The treasure exuded a musty, pungent smell; I half expected Sam

Bellamy to appear in wavery lines above the bed, like a genie from a bottle, and give me a salute. But I had one-upped Bellamy; I had the treasure *and* Heidi.

Uncle Bill, I thought, would have loved this.

SQUALLS

THAT FIRST FLUSH OF SUCCESS lasted about another half hour. Then the phone rang.

I grabbed it and answered softly.

"Congratulations," Birgitta said. "I'm sorry to call so late, but I tried earlier . . ."

"We were at the Land Ho." We hadn't been speaking much; I was surprised she made the gesture.

"So this is really it. After all—"

Heidi said, "Who is that?"

I missed whatever Birgitta had said.

"I really appreciate you calling," I told her. "I know Brandon wants to get out on the boat; if you'd like to see—"

Heidi jumped up onto her knees. "What's going on?"

Birgitta asked, "Is something wrong?"

"No, noth—"

Heidi reached over me and grabbed the base of the phone.

"Jesus, Heidi."

She stopped just long enough to glance across the room. Before I could stop her the phone went flying, stopped short of my dresser mirror by the cord plugged into the wall. As the receiver skittered across the floor, a tiny voice said "Barry?"

Obviously, Heidi didn't want Birgitta in this house, back in my life.

"She just called to congratulate me," I told her. And when she didn't have an immediate answer for that: "This isn't the time to go crazy—we're past the hard part."

In retrospect, that was a great moment of naïveté. I had found the *Whydah,* something generations of Cape Codders had dreamed of doing, and the romantic in me could celebrate. But there was still plenty of work to do, and when it was over I'd look back at those first years, the years of the search, as the good old days.

The storm couldn't keep us on shore for long. Not only did everyone on the crew want to work as much as possible, but it seemed as if half the world wanted to join us. Bob Lazier and Mickey Salloway flew out the minute they'd heard what we found. There wasn't room for everyone who wanted to be on the *Vast* if we were going to get any work done, but the good news gave my credit a boost; we got an advance on gas to shuttle people out and back. On the deck of the *Vast,* they crowded around the monitor.

Underwater, gold and silver waited.

We had grown used to the dimness under the surface, the swirls of sand and mungweed. Diving despite my bad ear (if the hearing was lost, it was lost; I could survive a spinning bedroom for this), I'd scan the pit. After a year of seeing nothing but sand and rocks and worthless junk, it was amazing to see, as if they had been sitting here waiting for us, clusters of coins in the open. I'd gather them by the handful, collecting them in a canvas diver's bag; when I picked up all I could see, I'd move a rock and find more. I saw the Spanish cross on the back—the image that had burned into my mind as I rubbed that first coin, the image I'd see for years whenever someone asked me about finding the treasure—and I knew I was holding another coin from Bellamy's cargo. The silver had turned slate gray with oxidation, but the gold we found was as brilliant as it had been the day Bellamy's quartermaster, Noland, counted it carefully into shares. Gold dust lined the sand like wrinkles of butterscotch; after trying to scoop it up only to see it filter through our fingers, Beyer went back on board and returned with an old turkey baster we used to prime the engines and a plastic sandwich bag left over from someone's lunch.

This wasn't the sort of wreck that yielded a little here, a little there; we logged up to thirty dives a day, bringing up as much as we could

Clifford's boat, the *Vast Explorer II*, a twin propeller diesel of white oak. It would take the ruthless pounding of the Atlantic Ocean which had worn rugged cliffs into Marconi Beach. *Maritime Explorations, Inc.*

Barry's Uncle Bill as a young man, hunting on the cape. Bill's lusty tales of the *Whydah* wreck inspired Barry to become a part of the legend. *Barry Clifford*

A contemporary rendering of the *Whydah* galley by artist John Batchelor, based on research performed at the wreck site. A part of cape lore, the three-masted galley measured one hundred feet or more and was rated at approximately three hundred tons—a worthy prize for Captain Sam Bellamy. *The Whydah Joint Venture*

Only Stretch matched the size of the mailboxes, used to blow holes under water. The cages on the mailboxes proved awkward and noisy and were later removed altogether. *Maritime Explorations, Inc.*

The crew confer. LEFT TO RIGHT: Trip Wheeler, Bruce Etchman, Stretch, Barry, McClung, Levin, Chris Polopolous. *Maritime Explorations, Inc.*

Diver Todd Murphy wears a Viking dry suit for a dive in the cape's icy ocean waters. Dry suits warm the diver by keeping water from touching the diver's skin and allowing him to wear special insulated undergarments. *Maritime Explorations, Inc.*

Heidi Pearl on the deck of the *Crumpstey*, surrounded by magnetometer equipment. *Bill Dibble, Maritime Explorations, Inc.*

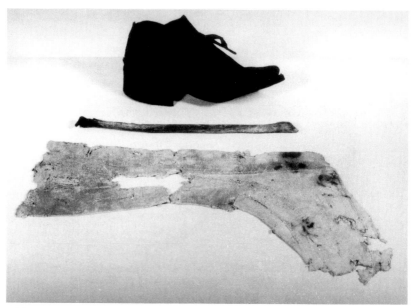

Although unusual for organic materials to be salvaged, this shoe, bone, and sock were discovered in concretion. The concretion helped to protect them from centuries under sand and salt water. It is believed this leg wore the sock and shoe and belonged to a man of short stature, probably no taller than five feet four. *The Whydah Joint Venture*

These brass and silver buckles were used for shoes, belts, and garters. The distribution of these items on the site helped to interpret the social status of pirates on the *Whydah*—with silver centered at the stern and brass centered at the bow. Even pirates had a hierarchy of command on ship as officers lodged aft and common sailors forward. *The Whydah Joint Venture*

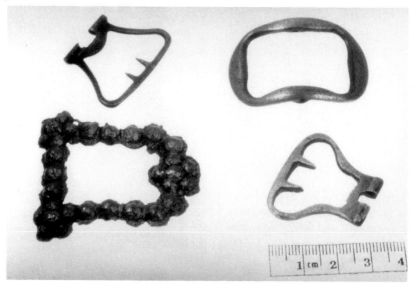

Sampling of shot. The most numerous artifact recovered from the wreck, shot was found all over the ship in eighteen or nineteen different sizes, but was mostly concentrated in the back half of the vessel. *The Whydah Joint Venture*

This leather ammunition pouch, which was found holding twenty-eight lead shot (or bullets), had wooden inserts to keep it stiff and a silk ribbon tie. The find corroborates a late seventeenth-century record indicating that Henry Morgan, a great buccaneer, sent a pouch with thirty lead shot to the Spanish colonial governor of Panama as a gift. *The Whydah Joint Venture*

Louise DeCesare carefully chips the surface of a cannon, at least 275 years old, at the lab. At right are pewter dinner plates fused to the cannon barrel. *Sherwood Landers*, Cape Cod Times

Artifacts are coded and catalogued at the *Whydah* lab. *Greg Derr*, The Patriot Ledger

Barry's father, Bob Clifford, working in the lab on the restoration of a sword hilt. *Barry Clifford*

Restored sword hilt and filigree decoration, once brandished by a *Whydah* pirate. *The Whydah Joint Venture*

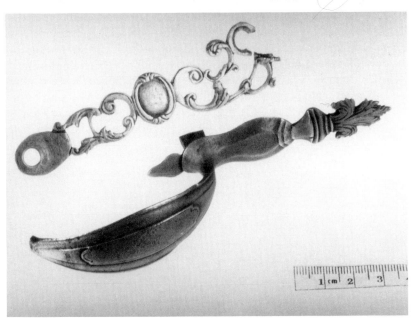

Navigational tools, highly prized by the pirates, were either used or traded. These were found clustered at the stern. *Shown:* The ring dial, invented between 1589 and 1618 by Edward Wright, was used with a compass or alone, to ascertain the time of day or to determine the altitude of the sun when figuring latitudes. The dial is marked with letters to coincide with months, and numbers that represent hours of the day. These symbols are inverted to measure northern or southern latitudes. The two brass sectors measure distance and angles, and were used to make calculations for gunnery or navigation. The blunt-end compass, used for drawing, is marked with the initials of its maker. A pointed compass, also called a divider, is pictured at the far right. *The Whydah Joint Venture*

carry. One morning, before the rest of the crew arrived, Stretch and Beyer came up with 800 coins. Another day I brought up 280 in twenty minutes. We found 3,000 coins in the first days after the discovery. In order to catalog them, we'd lay them out in lines across the gunwales according to denomination and metal, sunlight dancing off their surface.

Raising the gold dust was more complicated. We used a piece of equipment called an airlift to remove heavy materials, moved rocks and layers of sand with our hands, and sucked up the thinnest wrinkles of gold with the turkey baster. It worked as well as anything else we found.

Why had we missed this lode for so long? The weather. I had miscalculated how far offshore the *Whydah* lay. The wind and waves had been eroding the cape, and I underestimated their power. In 1717, according to Southack, the *Whydah* sank approximately five hundred feet from shore. By 1984, the cliffs had receded a thousand feet, or nearly two-tenths of a mile. Also, the *Whydah* sank in about thirteen feet of water. Due to erosion of the ocean floor and a significant rise in sea level, the same spot was now under eighteen to twenty feet of water.

We left the cannon where they were, partly to mark the spot, partly because we needed to decide exactly how to go about raising and transporting them—and I didn't think they'd fit under my bed. We didn't worry about them being covered over with sand; we had the spot charted on maps, marked with a buoy, and burned into our memories. If we disturbed them, though, a cache of coins or gold dust that wouldn't register on the magnetometer might easily be lost.

Of course, that's only one way gold can disappear.

In *Treasure Island*, Dr. Livesey warns, "Look out for squalls when you find it." Our first squall blew up on an apparently sunny day; Rob came over to me and said quietly, "I want to talk to you."

His tone made it clear something was seriously wrong. I left a reporter from *Life* magazine staring at the monitor and followed Rob to where the crew kept their packs of personal items on the *Vast*. He knelt, reached into one of the bags, and pulled out some coins.

"Whose is that?"

"Kaplow's. He's been slipping these under his wet suit."

"I'll kill him."

Rob shook his head. "Don't say anything. I've got it under control."

Gordon Kaplow was a burly, red-bearded guy who had worked for years with another salvor I knew. During the winter I had run into Kaplow in Boston, told him what I was doing, and ended up hiring him.

In retrospect, I should have been more careful. Kaplow had worked for some environmental organizations, which was fine by me, but one day he actually said, "I could much more easily kill a person than an animal." I assumed he was exaggerating to make a point, but Kaplow had a strange sense of humor; he'd give a big barrel-chested laugh to things none of the rest of us found funny. He had plenty of experience diving, though, and when I ran into him I wasn't sure what kind of crew I was going to have in the spring.

I asked Rob, "You think anyone else is in on it?"

"I've been watching. It's just him."

Without revealing anything, I called for a meeting of the entire crew at The Barracks. Rob rode over with Gordon, making sure he didn't lose sight of the bag.

Maybe the crew noticed Rob and I were distracted, not joking around; whatever the reason, they were unusually quiet. Once everyone was there, sitting and standing around the room, Rob said, "Okay, Gordon. Put your bag on the table."

Even guys who didn't like Rob didn't talk back to him; he was too big, too imposing.

Kaplow set the bag on the table.

"Show us what's in there."

Kaplow pulled out a pair of pants and a shirt, then a spare face mask and a few other things.

"You're forgetting something," Rob told him.

"Look," Kaplow said, "this is a mistake. I never—"

"Never thought you'd get caught," Rob said.

When Kaplow finally reached into one of the pants pockets and held out the coins, the rest of the crew blew up; if Rob and I hadn't been there, they would have torn the guy apart.

"You've got twenty minutes to pack your stuff and get out," Rob told him. "If I see you around the *Whydah*, it's your ass."

Kaplow packed and left. We never saw him again.

The next squall that blew up had been on the horizon a long time. After we found the treasure, and especially after firing Kaplow, Rob asserted himself over the others more than ever. He justified it, I'm sure, from experience; where there was one thief, there were bound to be more. But Rob got carried away.

One night Beyer and Stretch slept on the *Vast* so they could start work as soon as the sun rose, without waiting for the rest of us. I tried to discourage them—it was risky not having anyone above the surface if anything went wrong—but after all the months of frustration they were too excited to sit still. By the time the rest of the crew arrived on the *Crumpstey* the two of them had already lined up almost a hundred coins on the gunwale.

Instead of saying hello, good work, or anything else, McClung pointed to Stretch and said, "Check him for coins."

Stretch smiled.

But Rob was serious.

"Why is it you two guys are so anxious to start diving?" he said. "How many coins have you really found?"

Stretch stood tall. He cast a shadow over Rob. "You can walk over here and count them."

Beyer told Rob, "Don't be an asshole."

Todd Murphy told me later that he saw Stretch's arm jump; he was that close to going after Rob. It would have been like two giants fighting.

When he saw nobody was going to support him, Rob backed off—but the fuse had been lit.

A week after I brought up the first coin, the state Board of Underwater Archaeological Resources held one of its best-attended hearings ever at the Peabody Museum in Salem. Dr. Paul Johnston, representing the museum, took a moment to welcome everyone. "I'm delighted to see such a degree of interest in underwater archaeology," he said, then left a sign-up sheet for people interested in a conference on the subject to be held the following January—

—which was a joke. The *Whydah* was the only reason the museum was crammed with people and reporters, and the board knew it. They congratulated me, said they felt the discovery was "significant," and made it clear they wanted to work with me in whatever way they could, beginning with providing security for the site. As if that wasn't enough hypocrisy for one day, later in the meeting the board told the press Costa and Bill Daniels had made an "exciting" discovery of tin ingots on the *White Squall.* In other words, they had finally found what we had marked with a buoy the year before.

The only good news was that, since we couldn't sell treasure and artifacts from the *Whydah* until everything had been brought up, treated, and catalogued—assuming we'd want to sell it—and because Costa and Daniels had made a racket about the *White Squall* being historically significant, the board wouldn't let them sell any of the tin they had raised. It was nice to see somebody else squirming for a change.

(Meanwhile, Crockett reported to the board that the Old Blue Fishing Company's search of their site had turned up "one piece of wood that . . . indicated an old wreck." Which is like finding a penny and claiming to have discovered evidence of a bank.)

Then the board began new business. First on their list was to decide whether we had found the *Whydah.*

"What are you talking about?" None of them looked me in the eye; Joseph Sinnott kept talking. I asked Allan, "What are they talking about?"

Jim Bradley, a member of the board and the Massachusetts Historical Commission, looked down his nose and said, "It's an early wreck, it's an important wreck, it has some of the same characteristics as the *Whydah* may have. But to say it's the *Whydah* is premature at least. That area of the cape has one of the highest densities of shipwrecks of any place on the East Coast. There are hundreds and hundreds of wrecks out there."

"What were you just congratulating me for?" I asked the board. "What was all that talk about security?"

Softly, Bob Cahill said, "There's no doubt you've found an important wreck, which might very well be the *Whydah*. Some of us, though, feel we should wait for further evidence before making formal recognition."

The ghost of the *General Arnold* cast its long shadow; the board didn't want to get burned again. Talking to Cahill later, I realized the board members themselves disagreed. Even the ones who thought we had the *Whydah* couldn't decide if they had the authority to verify the discovery, or how much evidence they should require. An outside self-styled "expert," who contributed to picture books about Northeast shipwrecks, said, "If they came up with a quarter-board that says 'Whydah,' then I would believe them." The quarter-board, along with the rest of the wooden ship, had probably become a part of somebody's barn as soon as Southack left the cape. The state board might just as well have asked for a videotape of the wreck.

If these people had done their homework, they would have known there was no other shipwreck from the *Whydah* era fitting her profile anywhere near the spot I was diving.

"Either I've found her," I said, "or I found the wreck of a boat carrying a pirate museum."

The board then delivered even worse news.

"The only way to answer this doubt satisfactorily," the chairman said, "is to conduct a full archaeological examination of the site before another coin is disturbed. Such an examination is the responsibility of Maritime Explorations."

I was stunned. This was an expensive and time-consuming complication.

The meeting ended the way almost every board meeting ended; Costa and Crockett headed straight for the press. I couldn't wait to read tomorrow's paper.

I turned to Allan. "Aren't we suing these people?"

"It takes time. Everything takes time."

Understand this: none of us doubted. None of the investors, none of the divers, none of my kids, no one. Even Costa and Crockett knew they were beaten, though they weren't about to admit it. Treasure from an anonymous wreck, they knew, would be a lot less valuable than the treasure from the *Whydah*. The self-proclaimed experts who doubted us had a different motivation; they used their credentials to cover their bullheaded insistence that private salvors simply couldn't succeed. They demanded the kind of regulations that had created pirates in the first place. Then there were people who had to believe we hadn't found the *Whydah* just so they could keep telling stories about the treasure that was never found.

Within a week, the Boston papers and wire services carried more stories questioning the validity of our find. No one argued the authenticity of the artifacts; they just weren't convinced they were from the *Whydah*. And once the press picks up what it calls a "good" story, the truth can be buried, especially if the explanation is too subtle to explain in a simple sentence.

Of course, there was no way I could finance an archaeological expedition. Despite all the treasure, we were cash poor; our original investors were looking for returns, not more expenses. We couldn't begin to sell anything we brought up until it had all been thoroughly documented—and we couldn't document it until we had done the full archaeological report and raised the rest of the treasure. And even if we found a way out of that Catch-22, we still couldn't do anything with the treasure until our lawsuit against the state was decided and we learned how much of it was ours.

Just when everything should have been coming together, it was collapsing. I couldn't pay the crew, I couldn't dive, and I couldn't afford to hire the top-rank archaeological team I needed. There was no escaping with Heidi; after that phone call from Birgitta she had started a familiar complaint: I spent too much time on the boat and with the press, even with my children.

There was no choice but to try to find solutions. I called Lazier, who had returned to Colorado.

"We can't do a damned thing," I told him. "Can't we find the money somewhere?"

"We could kidnap Donald Trump and hold him for ransom." (This was back when Trump had money.)

Lazier realized we'd never see a return on our investment until we satisfied the board; he managed to come up with another $50,000.

That wasn't enough to get us far, but in August we hired a company called the Maritime Archaeological and Historical Research Institute. This was one of the first times a private salvor had ever contracted with professional archaeologists under the Code of Ethics and Standards of Research Performance of the Society of Professional Archaeologists—which is another way of saying the board was making life difficult for us in ways no one else had even thought of. So although not a member of SOPA, the Institute had to follow SOPA standards. Compliance with the state and federal guidelines would eventually transform our treasure hunt into an underwater dig of historic significance. All the same, our men wanted to kill each other.

The archaeologist, Riess Warren, initially assumed that the artifacts we had discovered lay more or less in the same relative position they had settled into in 1717. Much later we learned that sand in the location was being completely replaced every fifty to sixty years, and in the *Whydah*'s day had been replaced every thirty-five to forty years. But even then we knew that, as much as the bottom shifted, there was no way the artifacts could have remained where they had fallen. The heaviest objects eventually fell to the rock and clay level of the ocean floor, while lighter objects shifted.

But what Riess wouldn't accept was what we had realized the first week of diving; the site wouldn't hold still while we worked.

So Riess took us back to square one by remapping the site and the objects in it according to the standard archaeological method. You've probably seen this on television: a group of sweaty people rope off a site somewhere in Egypt; they make a string grid to denote exact locations, carefully remove the artifacts one at a time, often dusting away at them with basting brushes, then photograph, sketch, and label them. The method works. But try that underwater off the cape and soon you'll be modelling those nice white jackets with the sleeves on backwards.

Riess literally wanted divers to lay cord over the sand.

"You know there's no way these guys can do this," Todd told me. "You might as well draw a grid with colored pencils."

"We have to let them try," I said. Otherwise, the board would say we weren't in compliance. The board had also required us to allow them to visit the site; now I wanted to force them to come out and watch this circus. It didn't help that I was paying Riess's outfit good money while my crew, who were now essentially working for Riess, could only hope their shares in the company would eventually be worth something.

As our divemaster that season, Todd did everything he could to set the grid in place and measure it with a tape measure. He'd shove a stake into the sand, tie the line to it, start to measure—and that entire part of the ocean floor would simply drift away. Riess insisted he could pinpoint the location of artifacts to within a quarter of an inch, but even on calm days, currents moved the line, mungweed caught on the tapes and twisted them . . . the whole thing was a disaster.

Somehow Todd managed to keep his sense of humor. It helped that Riess had a bad stomach. When the water got even mildly choppy he got sick, and in order to save face he'd try to do it privately. The crew took a certain pleasure in saying, "You okay, Warren? You want to sit down a few minutes?" He'd smile one of those pasty-green smiles and try to go back to work.

"Everything hasn't gone exactly as I'd planned," he told me one day, "but even our mistakes teach us something. It can be as valuable to learn which methodology fails as to discover which one succeeds."

Easy enough for him to say; he was failing on my dollar.

When I told Riess what he wanted couldn't be done, he referred me to a friend of his, another archaeologist, who said, "We once reconstructed a ship that exploded in a lake. We were able to reestablish the order of things right down to the sequence of jars in the spice rack."

"Right," Todd said. "But if they think we can do that here, they're a bunch of knuckleheads."

Fire marshals and bomb experts do that kind of reconstruction all the time—and under ideal conditions, it might have been possible in a lake. But the surf zone under the Atlantic Ocean is no bathtub.

Riess next talked me into constructing a contraption called a coffer dam: four steel panels joined to make an 8′ × 8′ square. Theoretically, when you set the coffer dam in the sand, the current can't move whatever's inside, and you have a hard surface to measure from. Divers work inside it, recording the exact locations of each piece of treasure. (But there was no treasure; not to these people. To them, everything was an "artifact." At lunch one day, Todd said, "Just think of the power. As I drink from this can, it's a mere can. But I throw it overboard, and whammo—instant artifact.")

It was all the crew could do to keep from laughing out loud the day Riess's giant box went into the water. The bottom of the test pit was slightly smaller than eight feet square, so it took us all day to fit the dam inside. The next few days the weather kept us ashore. When we returned to the site, the coffer dam had disappeared.

Riess insisted we must have mischarted the spot, but after wasting most of the morning diving he finally let Todd look where he thought it should be—and there it was, buried under four feet of sand. Somebody suggested we make an even bigger dam—say, 16′ × 16′—lower it, get out the basting brushes, and treat the first dam as an artifact. Riess was not amused.

Even after we uncovered it, the dam was too small to work in. It got caught on every small rock down there, and since it wouldn't sit properly on the bottom, the current kept bringing sand back in, which of course defeated the purpose. In desperation, Riess's men started jamming any flat piece of metal they could find along the sides: old highway signs, a car hood, even aluminum siding. Adding insult to injury, by the time Riess was willing to give up, the dam was stuck, wedged into the rocks. Worse, it was so big, it acted like a beacon for the magnetometer, distorting the readings. As hard as we tried, it wouldn't budge. It's still out there, amusing the fish.

"Hey, Barry," Mikey Andrews said to me one day. "Let's get rid of these guys for a while. I'll give them Ivory over eggs for lunch."

Mikey claimed to have any number of special recipes designed as tools of revenge. More than once he had threatened to add a shot of liquid Ivory soap to someone's scrambled eggs—not enough to taste, but enough to keep the recipient busy in the head for the better part of the day.

"I'm shocked," I told Mikey. "I could never condone such behavior. Mr. Riess is a professional colleague of ours."

"Horseshit," Mikey said cheerfully.

After wasting some of the best weeks of the 1984 dive season—and $30,000—Riess and Maritime called it a day.

Nearly two months after we tied off to a cannon, we were finally allowed to bring up more artifacts, noting their precise location. In addition to coins, we uncovered gold bars, ingots, broken pieces of gold jewelry, cuff links, cannonballs, muskets (some with silk ribbons still attached; Bellamy and his men enjoyed the occasional flourish), navigational instruments, pieces of rigging, parts of swords, pewter plates, grenades, weights for measuring gold and chemicals, gaming pieces, scupper liners, a keg spigot, and more.

But we didn't know that.

What we actually brought up were large and small and medium chunks of stuff that looked like sand and rocks, some as big as four feet square. In order to find out what was inside, each concretion had to be x-rayed. Then, depending on what we found inside, various methods were used to ease the concretion away.

That couldn't happen until we had a full archaeological lab. The funds Bucky Zimmerman had begun raising in Minnesota the previous winter still hadn't materialized; until they did, we were keeping the treasure in an old warehouse protected by an armed guard.

The weather held, and on October 7 we were finally ready to bring up our first cannon. After carefully running straps around it and balancing the weight, we used a crane to lift the cannon to the deck of the *Vast*. We then took the *Vast* to a Provincetown pier, where a rented crane waited to lift the ton of iron into our pickup truck.

When we pulled into P-town, a crowd milled around; word had gotten out that something was going to happen. We tested the straps again, making sure nothing would slip, then hooked the cannon on. It rose slowly, then swung out over the deck.

As I headed for the pickup to help guide the crane operator, someone began running toward me: Matt Costa. From the look in his good eye, I could tell he wanted trouble.

"You salted the wreck!" he shouted. "You may be able to fool the rest of these people, but that thing's got barnacles on it."

"Get out of here," I told him. "This is private—we leased this area."

"You know it as well as I do—barnacles don't grow on a buried cannon."

"Just shut up." Over the years the cannon must have been exposed at times—but I wasn't in the mood to explain that to Costa.

He snarled, "Get outta my way." Pushing me back, he took out a camera and began snapping pictures of the cannon, still shouting so the crowd could hear. "He's a fraud! He screwed up the *Arnold* and now he's screwed up again!"

I lost it; jumping at him, I knocked the camera to the ground, shattering the lens.

Costa screamed for the police.

"If you don't get the hell away from this dock," I told him, "I'll throw you off it."

"What, you're going to cut me with that knife you wear?" he said. "You're not man enough to cut me, and you're not strong enough—"

I knocked his camera out of his hands and kicked it off the pier.

"Barry," Todd said, "cool down." He had come up beside me. Costa and I were chest to chest.

"You want to fight? I'll get my gun," Costa said. "Get out of the way." He kept walking as he talked. The crane had been moving all this time, but now Costa shouted something to the operator and the cannon stopped, suspended just above the bed of the pickup truck.

"Get it up," he said. "That's evidence!"

If he got the cannon, I'd never see it again. I jumped onto the bed of the truck, reached for my knife, pulled myself onto the crane's boom, and cut the cannon loose, dropping it onto the mattresses and old tires we'd laid down for protection.

Stretch and Beyer jumped into the cab. "Gun it!"

Costa had gone completely insane. As we took off, he and his boys gave chase in their car.

Provincetown is a fishing town, but it's popular with the tourists and the arts crowd because it's "quaint"; the buildings are jammed together, the streets so narrow you can walk from a Portugese bakery to a leather shop in about three steps. But the streets weren't safe for walking that day; we careened through them, screeching and dodging, sending pedestrians jumping back on the sidewalks. Behind us, riding in the passenger seat, Costa pulled out another camera. Meanwhile, every wild turn set the two-thousand-pound cannon rocking against the mattresses. I pictured the headline: "Treasure Hunter Cannon's Last Victim."

About that time, a police car pulled beside us.

"That man threatened me with a gun," I told the officer as he got out of his car.

"He's trying to swindle the state of Massachusetts," Costa said.

The policeman looked from me to Costa and back to me. "Get out of your vehicles. I want to see some identification from all of you."

"What I want to know," Stretch said later, "is how did you cut through that six-inch strap so fast?"

"Must have been adrenaline. And I keep that knife pretty sharp."

"Part of the job," Beyer said. "That's why you're the captain."

THE PROOF

On January 27, 1985, the *Whydah* made the cover of *Parade* magazine. From Boston to Iowa to San Diego, people dropped their Sunday papers on the kitchen table, picked up the magazine insert, and read about "the man who discovered a $400 million pirate treasure." Though it wouldn't affect the board, at least one national magazine was willing to accept that the ship we had found was Bellamy's. In the article, I explained that although everyone else involved wanted to sell it, the best place for the *Whydah* treasure would be a working museum where visitors could see the entire collection, learn what had to be done to preserve it and, most importantly, learn the truth about pirates.

The value of the treasure had always been the subject of speculation—and still is today. What's a ship full of gold and silver worth? On the most conservative end, you could melt down the metal and sell it (gold is, after all, worth its weight in gold). But all artifacts, from cannons to teapots, have historical value, and gold coins from the only documented pirate treasure ever to be raised are worth—

—whatever someone will pay for them. Similarly, a nonfunctioning pistol might get you a buck or two at a pawnshop. But Sam Bellamy's pistol, with silk ribbons still tied around the handle, would be priceless. So whenever anyone asked how much the treasure was worth, I told them it was invaluable. But the media had latched onto "$400 million." Typical reporters, bent on writing an arresting lead paragraph, only wrote down that figure.

Since we were treasure rich but cash poor, when people started calling, I listened. The Reagan-era boom had turned every kid with an MBA into a Wall Street millionaire—for a few years, at least—and pirate booty was as exotic and appealing to them as it had been to the original Colorado investors. Managing high-stakes finances can be complicated business; we weren't exactly getting checks in the mail. Still, the rash of publicity encouraged Bucky Zimmerman and his friends in Minnesota to send part of the million dollars they intended to invest.

It was time to do the job right.

We bought the dry suits and Aga equipment we'd been loaned the previous year. Todd Murphy built a surface-supplied air system that fed air to the divers from an on-board compressor, which meant no more clumsy tanks on their backs, no more regulators in their mouths. We also installed a communications system that included tiny microphones in the divers' masks, so we could talk to them, they could talk to us and, when things were slow, the divers could listen to Red Sox games while they worked.

To expedite the work itself, we replaced the turkey baster with a sluice to separate the sand from gold dust or other small artifacts on deck. Our plan for the upcoming season was to remove the sand overburden to within a foot of the artifacts, then have the airlift suck them up and the sluice clean them. That would eliminate any possibility that a random prop-wash blast might destroy something fragile.

On land, we put a healthy chunk of the rest of our new infusion of cash into a real laboratory. After years of watching professional archaeologists try to figure out how to describe the position of each artifact, Todd decided to pitch some ideas and a new solution was worked out. Instead of covering the surface under water with a string grid, we'd simply identify the precise location of one point. That point would then be the center of a grid we'd create on a computer. Each time we blew a hole we'd plant a temporary marker—usually a piece of half-inch pipe—and measure its distance from the central point. Then everything in that hole would be located with regard to that temporary marker, to the nearest foot.

"That's as accurate as we're going to get out here," Todd said.

The plan sounded right; it was simple, one of those things you're surprised no one else had thought of. But Todd writes software programs, and he had been giving the problem his attention for a long time.

"Just one thing," I said. "How do we fix that central point?"

Todd smiled. "The coffer dam. We've tried to pull it out, and it wouldn't budge. It's not going to drift anywhere. And no matter how much the sand moves over the winter, we'll always be able to find it with the mag."

With that solved, we could move a lot faster. Each object or concretion would be described and charted on a map of the site, then photographed and tagged once on the *Vast* and again upon delivery at the lab to assure that everything we found reached shore safely. The concretions would be assigned field numbers along with other identifying numbers, and all the information logged and stored.

The concretions were taken to the Arnold Greene Laboratory in Auburn to be x-rayed, so we could see what they held. Then, back at the lab, they were placed in a freshwater tank wired with DC current to leech corrosive salts from the metal and wood. In a matter of days or as long as years, depending on the size and composition of the encrustations, they would fall off, preserving the objects underneath. Concretions composed of multiple substances would have to be monitored closely, and objects such as textiles, which require less electrolytic current, removed from the tanks at the appropriate time. Finally, each object would be polished and covered with a protective coating of wax.

The new work space included a dry lab for drafting and photographing, a wet lab for small objects, a larger wet lab with holding tanks for larger concretions, and all the necessary electrical and water systems, as well as office space. What we built by August cost a quarter of a million dollars, and we still had to hire a conservator. Our new archaeologist, Bob Cembrolla, had plenty to keep him busy at the site.

We got unexpected help from Ken Kinkor, a graduate student at Illinois State University concentrating on pirate history, who turned out to be one of the most valuable people ever to work on the project. He had been writing his master's thesis on Bellamy's pal, Paulsgrave Williams, when he read about our work on the *Whydah*.

Understand, I was getting all kinds of letters—from people who wanted to invest, people claiming they had found the wreck years earlier, people who wanted me to find everything from lost planes to lost relatives, women who wanted to marry me, people who sent extensive genealogies demonstrating their blood relationship to Maria Hallett, and one man who suggested we excavate the site by surrounding it with rods filled with liquid nitrogen, creating a giant ice cube we could pop out of the ocean. But the details in Ken's letters convinced me his sails were good and taut. He already knew a tremendous amount about the pirates working the eastern seaboard; if he had access to everything we had found, he might be able to fit all the pieces of Bellamy's story together.

I invited him to the cape, and it's safe to say the crew knew he wasn't our new divemaster. Ken is tall and thin, with wild hair, pencils sticking out of his shirt pocket. He takes notes constantly, filling scraps of papers, even writing on his hand when he runs out of room.

"You really went to school to study pirates?" I asked him.

"As a boy I read the standard legends—Stevenson's *Treasure Island* and Edward Rowe Snow," he said. "As I got older, and kept reading, I saw there weren't many books about pirates that would pass as serious scholarship."

I needed a scholar on my side. "I want to flesh out the background of Bellamy, Hornigold, and anyone else who's in the public record. And we need to research the guns and ammunition and plates we've brought up to tie them to this period. When we're finished, I want to know everything we can about these pirates."

"It would be my pleasure to try," he said, smiling widely.

With that, the *Whydah* project had its own piratetologist.

"Hold it." I held up one hand. "There's something here."

Brandon and Jenny and I were walking through the scrub pines along the cliffs just before sunset.

"Is it treasure?" Jenny asked.

"I'm not sure, but . . ." I started sniffing. "Brandon—look over to the right."

Jenny shouted, "Me too, me too!"

"Here?" Brandon asked.

"Wait a minute . . ." More sniffing. "No, a little further ahead."

He came to a sandy spot beside a pine with just one limb. I had broken off the other two that morning.

"Try there."

He and Jenny began digging furiously, shoveling into the sand.

"I've got it, I've got it!" Jenny yelled. "It's a silver coin!" She showed it to Brandon, but when he reached out his hand she snatched it back.

"How did you know?" he asked. "How do you always know where the treasure is?"

A red band spread across the sky.

"Nothing to it."

Despite bad weather and occasional problems with our new equipment, we brought up 7,310 pieces of treasure that summer. Most were in concretions that had to be dissolved in the lab. In addition to more gold and silver, we brought up a smaller "kedge" anchor used for turning the ship around inside a harbor, musket shot, mercury for refining gold and silver ore, brick pieces of a stove, a handguard for a rapier hilt, and a gold ring with an inscrutable inscription: "Teye ba" on the face, and "W*F*S" on the inside.

My father enjoyed helping in the lab. "Bellamy's engagement ring?" he asked.

"We could never prove it."

One grisly find reminded everyone that we were dealing with more than inanimate treasure. The X ray of a concretion from beside a cannon revealed a human fibula, or lower leg bone, and a leather shoe. I was showing a reporter from the Associated Press around the lab when I noticed the concretion had dissolved, revealing something that hadn't been clear on the X ray: a long white stocking. Probably the poor guy was either crushed by the cannon or trapped in the rigging and drowned. I was struck by the smallness of his shoe—a size 6—and its tall black heel.

"The average height of Bellamy's men probably would have been about five feet four," Ken told us. "They were strong, but people were smaller then. Remember, too, most pirates were members of the lower class, so they didn't have the benefit of good nutrition. An upper class male would have been a good five inches taller."

An archaeologist told us the bone was an amazing find. "If it hadn't been concreted, it would have dissolved long ago. For the week or two after the wreck there would have been bodies washing ashore, then maybe some isolated parts of bodies worked free by the current, then eventually bones—a foot here, a hand there."

"Cheery thought," the reporter said.

Ken added, "Most of them would have been in their early to mid twenties. Since there were no vaccinations, most were pock marked, and no doubt they had their share of amputees."

"Why so young?"

"The average career span was about a year. Sailors at the time weren't well fed, and when their teeth fell out they weren't able to chew the ship's bread. Medical care was primitive, so it was possible to die from something as simple as an infected cut. The officers may have been in their thirties. My guess is, Bellamy was twenty-nine when he died."

A few days later, that pirate's leg bone made *The New York Times*.

As the word continued to spread, I made promising contacts. A friend of mine suggested that I meet a New York oil man with an interest in archaeology and a case of treasure fever.

"I'm a gambler," he told me when we met. "I'm in the oil business. I had twenty-three straight dry holes before I found one that paid off."

"We haven't brought up a tenth of the *Whydah*'s treasure."

But he had another project in mind.

In 1780 the British learned that General Washington's army was set to invade New York. The invasion never happened, but the British were scared enough that they loaded the H.M.S. *Hussar* with eighty American prisoners and £960,000 sterling intended to pay British troops. On November 23, 1780, she sailed up the East River, hoping to escape to Long Island Sound and then Newport, Rhode Island.

She never made it. When the ship reached the treacherous current at Hell's Gate, the wind dropped, and the river became unnavigable. The *Hussar* then hit an obstacle called Pot Rock, which knocked a hole in her hull. Carried swiftly north by the current, she grounded on the shore of present-day Port Morris, the Bronx, on the north side of North Brother Island.

Some people estimated the value of the coins at $500 million; beyond that, though, was historical interest. The British had escaped the wreck, but early accounts indicated that they left their American prisoners to drown. For years after she sank, people could see the masts jutting above the waterline. It drove them crazy to have that kind of treasure so close but unattainable. The British tried twice, and even Thomas Jefferson tried to salvage her.

I thought about it for a while, but I couldn't leave the *Whydah* until the doubts were behind us. Besides, there was still a lot of work to do; this was no time to walk away.

The oil man understood. "When you're ready to move on, give me a call."

A few years earlier, an outfit called Sub-Sal, Inc.—located, ominously enough, in Nevada, a state as well known for its lack of oceanfront property as for its gambling—received a license to recover the *deBraak*, a 190-year-old British warship that sank a mile off the coast of Delaware in a sudden storm in 1798. Legend had it that the ship, built by the Dutch, carried millions of dollars in gold and silver.

The job was a disaster. Sub-Sal made no effort to map or preserve the site and, when they got impatient, came up with a terrible idea: they'd rent a derrick barge, tie ropes and cables around the sunken ship, and raise the entire thing in one haul.

Testifying before Congress, J. Jackson Walter, the president of the National Trust for Historic Preservation, described what happened: "Lifted by cables without benefit of a proper cradle, salvors ripped into the hull and dropped much of its contents and interior onto the sea floor. The salvor then employed a clamshell bucket to dump the remains of the vessel into a road construction rock sorter to sift for treasure." The *deBraak* fiasco only strengthened every academic's bias against private treasure hunters. Walter concluded, "As a nation, we would not tolerate a commercial enterprise that bulldozed Gettysburg and then dumped the remains through a sifting machine to recover any valuable object. Yet this is exactly what current law allows treasure hunters to do to our nation's maritime legacy."

As it turned out, beyond the artifacts typically found on ships, the *deBraak* contained no significant treasure—at least, none that survived the salvage effort. What made the *deBraak* significant is that it inspired politicians around the country to tighten the screws on salvors. And as the early news of what was happening got around, I realized I was going to have to keep playing ball according to other people's rules.

So instead of bringing up more of the treasure, and possibly the undeniable evidence that we had found the *Whydah*, we spent a lot of our time satisfying the board and the Army Corp of Engineers by digging test pits far from where the treasure lay, simply to prove it wasn't there. The work was slow, dull for those of us who had been at it for three years and could point to the rest of the treasure, and discouraging for investors. No businessman wanted to hear we were going to spend the next year digging test pits.

One day in September we blew a twelve-foot pit about forty feet south of where we'd found the first cannons. After waiting for the sand to settle, McClung dove. A moment later he called up on his microphone, "There's something huge down here."

On deck, Stretch was wary. McClung's eagerness occasionally led him to overstatement, and he and Stretch weren't on the best of terms. Still, Rob had found a hull, and the original cannons . . .

"You're sure it's not a rock?" Stretch asked him.

"Jealous asshole." Rob's voice was distant and scraping from underwater, like an astronaut talking to Mission Control. "I think it's a bell."

Stretch rolled his eyes—but this time, I trusted Rob.

"Let's see if we can't dust it off."

Stretch revved the engines, but the propellers wouldn't blow any more sand away. The rest of the job would have to be done by hand.

Visibility was terrible; clumps of mungweed hung suspended in the water. I swam down toward the pit, then made out Rob.

"It's right below where I am now," he said, pointing.

I reached out, expecting to feel a concretion in the sand banks of the pit, but I saw it first. Lying on its side, half-buried, was the distinct half-moon shape of a ship's bell. Of course, we couldn't tell how old it was, and even if it had been on board the *Whydah,* it wasn't necessarily the *Whydah*'s bell; pirates stole everything. For all we knew, Bellamy's crew had fifty bells. It would be my luck.

You can't just dig your hands under a concreted ship's bell and carry it to the surface; we needed to run straps around it. When I went up and told the crew, Stretch and Beyer were like kids on Christmas morning.

"Bull's-eye," Beyer said.

Stretch added, "Let's get her up here."

Bob Cembrolla nearly jumped out of his shoes. "You can't do that. We've got to map the area."

Beyer said, "How long do you think this weather will last? By the time you've finished screwing around down there, it'll be winter. I'll be damned if I'm going to wait until next year to see whose bell that is."

I stepped between him and Cembrolla. "You should know better by now. We can't do the project right ninety percent of the time. If we just pull things from the site, we risk ruining everything."

I looked at Stretch for support; he didn't answer.

Rob had come up the dive ladder and stood beside me. "He's right, you know. I hate it, but he's right."

The measuring and mapping and recording took three years. At least, that's what it felt like. When Bob finally gave us the go-ahead, the surf was too rough for safety; when good weather came, we had to blow the pit again, and the mailboxes began to crack from the strain of a long season.

The first day we were ready to pull the bell up, one of the investors pointed out that it would be a good idea to have a television camera on the scene, just in case. So we waited a day and made some calls. CBS News sent a team to cover the story, but before they even reached the cape an earthquake shook the other side of the world.

On October 7, I decided to go ahead and get the thing out of the water before we lost our chance. Besides, if I brought up a bell that turned out to say "Gastonia," or "Elizabeth," the press would eat me for lunch.

Thanks to our experience with cannons, we raised the three-foot-long concretion with relatively little trouble. In the lab X ray, the bell itself appeared to be about two and a half feet tall and two feet wide, with a long, graceful neck and flared bottom. The rest of the concretion held coins, nails, pins, buttons, pipe stems, a file and chisel, bottle fragments and cordage.

"It's definitely eighteenth century," Cembrolla said. "The shape of the bells of that era is distinctive."

There wasn't much we could do. We set the entire mass in a tank of fresh water, turned the current on, and waited for the encrustations to loosen.

On the day before Halloween—the day dead spirits roam free, wreaking havoc—I got a call from the lab.

"You better get over here," Carl Becker, the lab conservator, said. "No one's touched the bell, but some of the concretion fell off in the bath, and we can make out a word: *Gally*. Without the *e*."

"What does that mean?"

"It means somebody couldn't spell." Then: "I'm not sure. But that's what it says. And you can see the bottom of what look like numbers, probably a year."

When I got to the lab, Carl and McClung and Ken and Tuck Whitaker, a neighbor and investor, were waiting for me. No more of the concretion had loosened; we could keep waiting, or we could speed the process along.

I asked Carl, "What are the chances of us doing any damage if we chip away at it?"

"To a bronze bell?" he said. "You'd have to whack it with a hammer."

So Brandon and another one of Carl's helpers began working with dental picks, concentrating on the edge of the concretion. Between the partially exposed numbers and the word *GALLY* was a small decorative Maltese cross.

Fifteen minutes crawled by—tick tick *tunk*, tick tick tick. Waiting,

I was struck by the range of force we had used during the excavation, from prop wash strong enough to blow through tons of sand to this delicate tapping.

Gradually, like the past itself rising through the watery blur of a dream, the date became clear.

1716.

"Is that it?" Tuck asked.

"Anything else she'll tell us," Carl said, "is still under that crust."

"It could take days to get that off with the picks," Rob said. Then: "I guess we just let the tank do the work."

Not a chance. "Hit it right there," I said, pointing at a spot just above where the concretion had started separating from the bell casing. "If you hit it there, that whole piece of crap covering it will just fall away."

One gentle hammer tap on a small chisel was all it took. The last layer of sand and corroded iron fell off in a five-inch chunk, leaving only dried salt on the words that completed the legend:

THE + WHYDAH + GALLY + 1716

Finally—evidence no one could deny. Not the board, not Costa and Crockett, not the newspapers, not the locals who didn't want to believe an "outsider" had found Bellamy's ship, not the academics.

"It's time for some people to eat crow," I said. "Call CBS and NBC. Call *The New York Times* and the *Globe*. And let's get somebody from the board down here."

"I can hear them already," Rob said, pointing to the legend. "They're going to say it's a different *Whydah*."

No one dared—but we had been wrong about one thing.

The ship, like others of its era, had been named after its main port of call—in this case, Ouida, a coastal community established by the French as a slaving port in what is now the West African nation of Benin. In the historical documents we had come across any number of variants, but the most common one—the name on my license plates, and the crew's T-shirts and caps, and our stationary, and all the legal documents—was "Whidah."

"Carl," I said, "call the printer. Tell him to change the spelling on the new prospectus."

"Forget the prospectus," Tuck Whitaker said. "What about my tattoo?"

TELLING THE TALE

A YEAR LATER, ROB AND I stood in a hotel in Denver. Specifically, we were in a hallway outside one of those nondescript conference rooms in which so much American business is conducted, waiting to make the most important presentation of all.

"You're sweating," Rob said.

"Am I?"

"There's nothing to worry about. The guys in there are just like you and me."

But he couldn't look me in the eye. I wore my old blue blazer and a worn but freshly pressed pair of khakis; everyone inside was wearing tailor-made suits. As for Rob, his hands gave him away, hanging out of his jacket like weapons.

Finding the bell ended any debate over the identity of the ship, but it hadn't leveled my mountain of debt. The more attention we got, the more scrutiny we were under; the lab staff kept growing, and work on the water kept moving more slowly. At one point we were told the company had to take out insurance on the entire crew, and after doing some shopping I found a policy with an annual premium of $100,000.

The one good thing about all the aggravation was that the *Whydah* project had been recognized as a breakthrough, one of the first and largest joint efforts of a private salvor and professional archaeologists. An internal memo from the National Advisory Council on Historic Preservation to the Army Corps of Engineers urged them to help us produce a report on our methodology so it could be duplicated in other corps districts.

That didn't much matter to the people sitting inside the conference room, the regional directors of what was then E. F. Hutton, the brokerage house. For weeks people had been telling me stories of how viciously they scrutinized potential deals. As an investment, the *Whydah* was "sexy" (that's the way those people talk, trying to make their work sound interesting). Somehow I had to convince them that our project, a risky proposition that devoured money, was in fact a guaranteed cash cow.

As I thought about it, I started talking aloud. "Why aren't we rich?"

"What?" Rob said.

"That's what they're going to say. 'If you're sitting on all this pirate treasure, why aren't you rich?' "

"These guys know business," Rob said. "They understand about development money and overhead."

"This is crazy. Would Sam Bellamy have done this? Can you see him typing up annual reports? 'This season featured over fifty hostile mergers, leading to the acquisition of thirty—' "

"Barry. We're not pirates."

While the Hutton directors spent over an hour tearing into a perfectly sensible, excruciatingly dull investment proposal for a Holiday Inn, I paced the hallway, deciding how much to tell them.

We had kept diving through the '86 season, which meant spending money we didn't have. In addition to coins, the concretions we took to the lab yielded four more cannons; "bar shot," or dumbbell-shaped cannon shot used to destroy rigging of a fleeing ship; swords and blades used in close combat once the pirates boarded the ship; hand grenades, which they used to flush sailors who fought from their cabins; three five-foot-long muskets; and more jewelry. Dr. Martha Ehrlich, an assistant professor of art and design at Southern Illinois University, Edwardsville, saw photographs of the *Whydah* treasure in *Art & Antiques* and identified the jewelry as African, specifically Akan. The Akan destroyed the jewelry whenever a new king took power, using the gold as money when trading slaves with the Europeans. The Akan jewelry on the *Whydah* predated any previously known examples by 140 years.

Rob Reedy, our new project archaeologist, had worked on the

deBraak. With the benefit of past experience, he insisted on meticulously following every procedure—from the way we identified what we found and recorded its location to the way we raised gold dust and smaller objects, using a Venturi hydraulic dredge. Unlike some of the other archaeologists who had come and gone, Reedy was a diver, so he had a better appreciation of the limitations imposed by our site. But he hated McClung from the start. The feeling soon became mutual. Eventually McClung lost his temper, vaulted to the *Crumpstey* over the rail of the *Vast,* and hit Reedy full force on the chest, knocking him flat on his back. It was a less than ideal working relationship.

Allan won our suit against the Board of Underwater Archaeological Resources; the Massachusetts Superior Court issued a restraining order prohibiting them from issuing any new permits near the *Whydah* site, or extending my competitors' existing permits. It was as if the judge had seen for himself the early board meetings; he said, "There may be more sharks in the courtroom than there are in the waters around the wreck."

That left two thorns in my side. The state of Massachusetts continued to fight for title to the *Whydah*'s remains and 25 percent of its value—as well as the authority to decide how the remaining 75 percent—my portion—was to be disposed of. While I had dealt with Costa and Crockett, the state turned out to be greedier, and far more dangerous.

The money raised from Minnesota had come and gone, and we were long past the days of scratching for donut money. I needed funding to support a huge operation: the lab, its staff, the divers, the rest of the crew, our growing battery of equipment, a larger salvage boat, historical experts, and lawyers. On top of that, I still fought to pay personal bills—for things as simple as food and heat—while Birgitta and I worked to establish the terms of our divorce. Whenever I tried to get money, bankers and investors pointed at my debt load; but whenever anyone wanted money from me, they pulled out the articles on the *Whydah* treasure and claimed I was a millionaire.

A few years earlier I had met Tom Bernstein on the Vineyard. He and his partner, Roland Betts, ran Silver Screen Management, Inc., which raised millions of dollars for Walt Disney motion pictures by means of limited partnerships comprised of thousands of investors contacted through Wall Street brokerage houses. Silver Screen had raised the money for virtually all Disney's films since 1984; in later years Betts and Bernstein became co-owners of the Texas Rangers. Although Roland had started from scratch in 1982, by 1986 he and Tom ran a large, lucrative operation.

Tom made it clear that no sane investment manager would encourage anyone to invest his children's college tuition in a sunken pirate ship. He and Roland are Ivy League products, entertainment lawyers, the kind of men who take *calculated* risks; like good casino managers, they know where they can make a little money, where they can make a lot—and they're paid to keep the odds in their clients' favor. They'd established something brand new in the Silver Screen partnerships, and in doing so worked to convince people that in a world of inexplicable hits and bombs, they knew how to steer a steady, reliable course.

When I first talked to Tom, I could tell he thought the project was fascinating but far too risky. Now that I'd found the ship's bell—and Mel Fisher had found the mother lode of the *Atocha* down in Florida and become a multimillionaire and media darling—the whole equation looked different.

"The *Whydah* satisfies our three criteria for investment projects," Tom told me. "It's fun, it could be very profitable, and it's got an unusual angle. That's where you come in. You're the man who can sell this."

Together they created a new limited offering called The Whydah Partners, L.P. The partnership would raise $6 million—enough to allow us to finish excavating and conserving whatever was down there. "We'll offer it to Hutton for their wealthiest clients," Roland said. "These are people who can afford to lose their entire investment—which, realistically, might happen." Bucky Zimmerman came down from Minnesota to work out the details. After years of fund-raising, I knew $6 million was going to come with enough strings attached to make me a marionette.

"What's the bad news?" I asked him. "How much of my soul do they want?"

Bucky said, "They insist on accurate, timely accounting. You'll have to tell them how you spend every dollar."

Another headache, but not an unreasonable request.

"And?"

"If you go over budget, there won't be anything they can do about it. They won't go back to the investors, they won't sell more shares."

Only a few years ago $250,000 had felt like a fortune. Now $6 million didn't sound like nearly enough.

Bucky continued. "When it's time to divide proceeds from the treasure, Whydah Partners will get eighty percent of the first $6 million, while you and your people will get twenty percent. With each succeeding $6 million, they'll get a little less, you'll get a little more. The proceeds will have to exceed $54 million before you get eighty percent."

Welcome to the big leagues.

"That's pretty stiff."

"We've gone over it; they feel that's the best deal they can offer and still encourage investors. They need to be able to show them how they'll recoup their initial investment and, if all goes well, show a profit."

I gave it a lot of thought. This deal wasn't going to do anything for my personal finances any time in the forseeable future; it meant giving them exactly what I was fighting to keep the state from taking. But if the worst failure would have been never to have found the *Whydah*, the second worst would be to find it and walk away leaving the job half done. The Whydah Partners would clear the project's debts and see it through to the end.

That's what brought me to Denver with Rob. This time, instead of sitting in Bob Lazier's panoramic condo in Aspen, we waited in the hotel corridor like busboys new on the job.

The door to the conference room opened. The poor slob representing the Holiday Inn deal, clearly heartbroken, looked like he had put everything he had on one last spin of the wheel—and lost.

Tom gave us a cheery smile. "Pirates, you're on."

Rob and I made our way to the conference room dias. The regional directors looked like store detectives waiting for us to get past the checkout counter before snapping the cuffs.

"I'm Barry Clifford," I said, "and what I'm going to talk to you about now isn't a T-bill or a shopping center or some hotel, like you've been hearing about all day. I'm here to offer you the chance to go on a great adventure. The goal is to find the long-lost gold of eighteenth-century pirates, and to write an important chapter in American history."

I took out a little pirate chest I'd found on the cape, flipped up the latch, and emptied the contents onto the lectern. You could hear the sound of the eyes of fifty regional directors popping out of their heads.

"These aren't chocolate coins in gold and silver foil," I told them. "These are from the *Whydah*." I held one up, letting it flash in the light. Rob carried two big handfuls to the front row for the brokers to fondle.

"In 1716, a young man named Sam Bellamy heard about the sinking of the Spanish Silver Plate Fleet south of what is now Florida. Bellamy had been a sailor; and in that day, sailors . . ."

I twisted Uncle Bill's Indian head ring around my finger as I continued. The brokers leaned forward.

". . . According to pirate testimony, I've only found a small percentage of the treasure that sank to the ocean floor in 1717. There's much more down there, and we know where, but I need your help to get it."

I had barely paused before a hand shot up. "Can somebody tell me when this deal's going to be available? I can sell all of it."

A second man shot up his hand. "Not so fast. I can sell this in a month."

Chaos. Before Roland and Tom could answer, the regional directors started fighting among themselves.

The private offering went on sale March 13, 1987; by May 14, all the units of the partnership had sold. Almost 40 percent of the investors were E. F. Hutton employees so excited about the investment that they never gave their clients a chance to buy into it.

Treasure fever must have blurred their vision; the Whydah Partners prospectus contained thirteen pages of such alarming "risk factors" as "The Ship May Not Be the *Whydah*"; "Quantity of Artifacts Cannot be Ascertained"; "Uncertain Market Value for

Salvaged Items"; "Role of the Commonwealth; Possible Claim of Key Artifacts"; "Sale or Disposition of Recovered Objects May Take Five Years, or More"; and "Risk of Total Loss."

None of that dissuaded the investing world from taking a gamble on a terrific bit of romance.

James J. Nixon is, I'm convinced, one of the great legal minds of our time.

In May 1987 Judge Nixon reached a decision, based on two keystones of admiralty law, on my suit against the state of Massachusetts.

Something called the "law of finds" governs the ownership of lost or abandoned treasure. Under the English rule that allowed Southack to claim the *Whydah* wreck for the Crown; all abandoned property belonged to the sovereign—the king or queen. In the United States, though, recovered treasure belongs to the finder unless one of two things happens: either the actual owner of whatever was found steps forward and proves he or she never abandoned it, or the federal government enacts what's called "an expression of sovereign prerogative"—that is, they have to claim, through law, their right to shipwrecks and their contents. The opinion, if I do say so, is one of the most entertaining legal documents ever written. It includes an eight-page account of the *Whydah*'s historical background outlining Bellamy's career, the fatal storm, and Southack's salvage efforts. Judge Nixon even quotes the "I am a Free Prince!" speech attributed to Bellamy by Defoe. Most importantly, he concludes that the Massachusetts legislature had in fact enacted an expression of sovereign prerogative—but they had done it improperly. (If you're dying for the details, I'll say this much: the Massachusetts statute drew its justification from the Federal Submerged Lands Act of 1953, which had been designed to give individual states control of natural resources, such as oil and mineral rights, within a state's three-mile offshore boundary. The *Whydah* wasn't a natural resource, the good judge decided, so the state statute was illegal. That meant sovereignty over the site was vested in the federal government, and under federal law at that time the ship belonged to me, the finder.)

Naturally, the state planned to appeal.

. . .

The media coverage didn't stop; if anything, it grew. Walter Cronkite, a Vineyard resident, did a segment for the CBS special *Walter Cronkite at Large*. At one point the cameras showed us lifting a cannon out of the water and onto the *Vast*'s deck, where gas bubbles started coming out of it. "You see those bubbles?" Cronkite asked viewers. "That's air that's been trapped inside this cannon since the moment it fell into the sea. It's the same air that the *Whydah* pirates were breathing just before they died, in 1717." He leaned down and inhaled, eyes marveling. "I can't believe it—I'm breathing 270-year-old air!"

The 1987 dive season was jinxed. I couldn't figure out any other explanation. Delays in refitting our new boat, coupled with the growing sand overburden (during the winter, the site had been buried under twenty-five feet of sand), kept us from doing much digging. The *Vast* showed serious signs of overwork. On top of that, the weather was terrible; and when the skies cleared, the seas were so churned up, sometimes fifteen feet high, that we couldn't work. During the entire season we weren't able to dive more than thirty days.

I felt trapped. The project had become enormous. Some days I thought I had become a suit—with a big staff and a lot of administrative responsibility. When I saw myself in an ad in *Esquire*, pitching shoes, I knew I had lost sight of the adventure I had set off on.

I spent most of the 1987 season in the lab in Chatham, where we had finally found the perfect flexible yet unflappable marine archaeologist. Dr. Chris Hamilton, officially our principal investigator, studied anthropology at Florida State, and at Pennsylvania State wrote his dissertation on underwater wrecks. He worked closely with George Fisher, a distinguished scholar who inaugurated a pioneering study of underwater archaeology and anthropology for the National Park Service. Hamilton's previous job had been as a "contract," or private archaeologist, so he was used to the tension between pure researchers and private companies working within fixed time and budget constraints to meet state and/or federal cultural resource management regulations. As Chris said, "Academics seldom if ever search sites in hopes of striking the 'mother lode.' " He pointed out, too, that while our failure to meet archaeological standards would give fuel to critics, our success would frighten academics who saw themselves losing control of their turf. No matter how hard they worked, he and all the other archaeologists who were associated with us at one time or another had a lot to lose in professional standing.

Todd Murphy's solution to the problem of identifying the location of artifacts, which Hamilton and Reedy concurred with, enabled Chris to produce a map showing the *Whydah*'s position when she sank and the distribution of her contents. In addition to being of historical interest, the map gave us useful information about the ship's final hours, and where to dig in the future.

At the lab, a staff of seven plus six volunteers worked magic on the concretions we'd pulled up. One day, like flowers from a silk hat, jewelry would emerge. Another day, navigational instruments, rope, an ornate rapier hilt, and a leather pouch. Some of the larger objects were going to take years to fully conserve. These included eight more cannon, large sheets of lead and, in a concretion $4' \times 5' \times 3'$ that the lab staff nicknamed "El Grande," a large section of rigging.

My son Brandon, who had spent the past summer with the crew, attacked lab work with the same enthusiasm. Under supervision, he picked away at concretions, getting covered in black sediment. He exposed one of our most remarkable finds: a fully intact pistol with a beautifully preserved brass handle decorated with a dragon and what appeared to be a Roman god, or "grotesque." In one of the concretions attached to a cannon we discovered another pistol—and from inside the pistol, wadded up, the lab technicians extracted pieces of paper. That required the attention of Gordon Harvey, a retired textile scientist, who worked a special brand of magic: by knowing the chemical properties of a variety of materials, and carefully experimenting, he was able to extract hemp, jute, cotton, flax, wool, and silk from formations as dense as a meteorite. His work on the paper revealed part of a letter; still legible were the words ". . . come we . . . of the 13th . . . at . . . note the . . . we are satisfied . . . before."

The letter was a rare find in part because of its age; paper wasn't a common commodity in the early eighteenth century. Steve Pope, an artist who drew renderings of artifacts for us, studied the scraps and determined that the pen was in good condition—there were no scratches on the paper which might indicate a worn or secondhand writing instrument—and that, combined with the penmanship, indicated the writer was probably a merchant. All of which, Ken Kinkor pointed out, was probably lost on Bellamy's men, most of whom would have been illiterate; to them, paper was the stuff you shredded and used for wadding. In this case, the pistol preserved the paper, but the paper also preserved the barrel of the pistol, which 'was on the point of collapse.

What we found didn't provide any earth-shattering insights into the world of piracy, but a lot of what had been educated guesswork was now confirmed by hard evidence. Most of the everyday silver—belt buckles, cuff links, buttons—had come from what appeared to be the stern, where the officers would have lived; the bow contained higher concentrations of brass, pewter, and gaming pieces. So while pirate ships were more democratic than merchant vessels, it seems there was still a clear hierarchy. Beyond that, everything we brought up from the ocean floor helped to humanize the pirates. When I saw the knife marks cut into pewter plates, I had a new appreciation for how hard and miserable their food must have been; when I saw knife marks in a gold bar, I realized they knew better than to trust the appearance of the riches they took.

Ken not only researched every new artifact the lab staff restored, but he continued his research on Bellamy. One day he made me a printout of his most recent work.

"This is just preliminary," he said. "There's a lot we don't know yet."

The printout listed forty-one ships Hornigold, Bellamy, and Williams had captured from January 1716 through April 26, 1717, including each ship's nationality; type; "master," or captain; the cargo taken by the pirates; and where it was overtaken. Ken was nothing if not thorough.

I told him, "I don't want you to leave tonight until I get full biographies of the crew."

Ken gave me an odd look, so I smiled: Ha ha. Little joke.

Then he shifted some books, dropped his pen and, stooping to pick it up, knocked a sheaf of papers onto the floor. Somehow he came up with what he was looking for. "I thought you had already seen this."

He handed me another list, this one headed "Known Piratical Associates of Samuel Bellamy." On it were biographies of the *Whydah's* crew. Culturally diverse, the list numbered Englishmen, Indians, Blacks, and Irishmen among it, each entitled to an equal share of the treasure after Bellamy had taken his own two shares—presumably from the best of the booty. Kinkor's work is dutifully reported in the 1988 *Annual Report of Archaeological Data Recovery*, coordinated by Hamilton, Kinkor, and the lab staff.

Introduced at least in part as a response to Mel Fisher's success and the *deBraak* catastrophe, the Federal Abandoned Shipwreck Act was working its way through Congress. The act would effectively transfer jurisdiction over shipwrecks in state waters to the states, legitimizing their attempts to claim title and at least some of the cargo. Allan called one afternoon to tell me the lawyers for Massachusetts planned to refer to the proposed federal legislation in their appeal.

Todd Murphy overheard the conversation. "Sounds bleak," he said.

I nodded. "If I had waited two years longer to get started on this . . ." Gone were the days of swimming to the site in a taped-up wet suit; gone were the days of storing treasure under the bed.

Winter was coming.

In January 1988 I went to New York's East River to search for the H.M.S. *Hussar*. The wreck lay under eighty feet of water—not terribly deep—within what contemporary reports described as a stone's throw from shore.

Unfortunately, some of those guys could really chuck a rock. The currents are still as serious a threat as ever—three hundred ships have sunk in roughly the same area—there are only one or two times a day, between tides, when it's safe enough to drop a diver, and the water might as well be liquid poison. The East River is teeming with benzene, PCB's, and a host of carcinogens, making it one of the world's most polluted waterways. Everyone who expected to come in contact with the water had been inoculated for every disease we'd ever heard of. Even so, each man had to step into a heavy dry suit with a special neck yoked to a Superlight hard hat, underwater mittens, and boots.

We devoted our first days on the water to looking at the bottom electronically, but that didn't get us anywhere: the East River is filled with so much ferrous metal that mag readings were useless, the bottom piled with so much junk it was hard to make out a distinctive profile.

With currents up to seven knots, each diver wore eighty to a hundred pounds of weights—about ten times the usual amount—to avoid being swept away. For the same reason, swimming was too risky—not to mention difficult due to the clumsy gear—so they had no choice but to crawl across the assorted garbage on the bottom: an enormous pile of discarded milk bottles from a long-gone Bronx dairy, part of a truck, more pier pilings, anchors, and a variety of worthless wrecks. Rob McClung fell through the deck of an abandoned barge. Later that day, while the divers were sprayed with a solution of bleach and water, then scrubbed with soap, Reedy and I looked through their booty bags.

He rinsed what looked like a brown stick about eight inches long. "A human bone," he said. "But I doubt it belonged to one of our American prisoners."

After a few months we'd had enough of battling the pollution and river traffic and current and zero visibility. We were more likely to lose someone's life than to find treasure. My divers were anxious to keep trying, but then we learned that the British government had heard what we were doing and claimed title to the ship.

In late March I said good riddance to the East River, and headed home to a sparkling spring on the cape.

As good as it felt to be back home, the 1988 season got off to a discouraging start. When it looked as if we'd be spending the foreseeable future blowing more empty test pits just to prove they were empty, John Beyer decided to attend to his insulation business. "This was the kind of work I came out here to avoid," he said. And Stretch said he couldn't work with Rob any longer; he was afraid of what might happen. "Either he goes or I go," he said. I tried to talk him out of it, but he had a family to support, and lobstering brought steady money with fewer headaches. "But listen," Stretch added. "If something comes up, and you really need me . . . you have my number."

Using a new boat the partnership funds had enabled us to buy, and with Todd in charge of all diving operations, Hamilton in overall charge of archaeology, and Reedy remaining as Field Director for archaeology, we accomplished the projected work of two seasons in just one. "I've been waiting for this," Todd told me halfway through the summer. "Now we're treasure hunters again." The crew was amazed at the size of the *Maritime Explorer*. Better still, the MEX rode like a yacht; we could bring people on board even in rough weather without making them sick. The new boat didn't have the soul of Gammage's *Vast*, but we had a table to eat at, a head that flushed with a handle instead of a pump and, amazingly, a button to push that automatically locked the mailboxes in place.

Now able to easily raise and store larger items, we returned to a spot where we had located cannons. Two of them were concreted together with what turned out to be two wooden barrels, a couple of muskets, and more ship's rigging. Our new crane lifted the entire mass and hoisted it onto the boat.

Piece of cake.

The artifact that got away—temporarily—wasn't the heaviest or the largest, but the most fragile. In one of the pits we discovered the ship's caboose, or stove—the same one Thoreau had been told could be seen jutting through the surface at low ebbs—concreted to a cannon. A cast iron and copper box roughly four feet by six feet, it should weigh about a ton. We cleared the sand and some debris from around the concretion, then put straps under it, but the metal, weakened by oxidation, threatened to collapse.

"Wait," I said. "Hold it."

Todd said, "We're losing our chance." The light rain that had been falling grew heavier; the sea began to churn.

"Let's think it through," I said. "Let's do this right."

Rob, waiting to dive back in, couldn't believe what he heard. "You've been hanging around too many archaeologists."

When the weather cleared, the stove was buried again, and before we redug the pit, we made another discovery. The site extended further to the northwest than we had thought, and a good-sized hit that we had assumed wasn't part of the wreck turned out to be the *Whydah*'s bow anchor. This was the big one—nine feet across the flukes—that Bellamy had used to try to hold the *Whydah* against the storm.

The anchor wasn't as dramatic a find as that first coin, or the gold, or the bell, but raising it was a big job. To have something that heavy up in the rigging is dangerous, and moving it is complicated. When we finally got the anchor on deck, I thought again about how well the crew responded to on-the-job training. After Todd's ankle injury that first year, we never had another serious accident.

"The *Whydah* must have been huge," someone said, admiring our newest artifact.

But I could only think of the storm. "Remember," I said, "this anchor didn't hold."

Christmas came early.

On the twelfth of December the Massachusetts Supreme Judicial Court, after having listened to both the state's appeal and Maritime's position, ruled that the *Whydah* belonged to Maritime. Judge Neil Lynch's justification was the exact legislation the state had hoped to use to make its case: the Federal Abandoned Shipwreck Act, passed that April, included a grandfather clause exempting legal proceedings brought prior to the law's enactment. The judge wrote, "The claim of the Commonwealth founders on the shoals of Federal sovereignty as surely as the *Whydah* foundered on the shoals off Wellfleet, ironically suffering the same fate as the 1717 proclamation of the Colony's Royal Governor, Samuel Shute, which claimed the wreck for the Crown."

Somewhere up there, Samuel Harding had to be smiling.

After finding the *Whydah*, it was my dream to establish a museum that would allow everyone—not just scholars or archaeologists or a few wealthy collectors—to see what we had discovered. Visitors would learn about the lives of Sam Bellamy and men like him who, for a variety of reasons, turned to piracy. The urge for freedom is a desire we still need to nurture; the sorts of conditions that drove pirates to murder and steal in the name of freedom still need to be fought. Visitors would also learn that the *Whydah*, originally intended as a slave vessel, ironically was manned by a multiracial crew, including at least twenty-five blacks—some estimates say there might have been as many as fifty—who lived together as equals. Perhaps never before has a time capsule come to us at a more critical moment.

I tried to pursue the leads quietly; by this time, the investors were asking when we were going to start selling all that gold and silver, all those priceless guns and pewter plates. Word got back to Bernstein and Betts—

—and they were all for it.

Everyone who learned about the *Whydah* was fascinated by it, and that fascination naturally led them to want to see what I had wanted to see: the tangible evidence of the ship's existence, and of Bellamy's career. Tom and Roland saw the value of keeping the treasure and artifacts together as a public collection. A museum could, after all, provide long-term revenue even greater than a one-time sale at Sotheby's.

After long negotiations, plans were created for a museum, featuring a full-scale re-creation of the ship—complete with a simulation of the fatal storm, a working conservation laboratory—tons of concretions, doubtlessly holding untold treasures, will be opened right before the public's eye, an exhibit on the *Whydah*'s early history as a slave ship, and , of course, the artifacts.

The bottom line: The museum would cost $70 million.

And I used to think $250,000 was a lot. Roland and Tom assured me that the museum could be financed and running by 1995.

With that new goal in mind, we reassessed all our activities. We had roughly nine thousand coins; a museum visitor wasn't going to be any more impressed, or informed, by the thought that we had thousands more that weren't on exhibit.

"That's not the point," I told Bernstein and Betts. "All our research shows we've only brought up a fraction of the treasure."

"If we're not going to sell the treasure," Roland interrupted, "the cost of locating and raising whatever might be left is an unnecessary expense. From what we can see looking at the mag surveys, the mother lode isn't there with the rest of the wreck."

Tom added, "For all we know, you've got all that's left. You said yourself that two hundred sixty-some years of storms have had their effect."

You've heard the advice before: be careful what you wish for, because you just might get it. Once they agreed to the museum, they turned their backs on the water. I had no choice but to end our work for the time being with the 1989 dive season, which we spent mapping the extended perimeter of the site.

Understand this, the mother lode *is* still out there. Think about it. We've only brought up several dozen cannon balls. I doubt very seriously whether men in the profession of piracy would go to sea with only a few pieces of ammunition per cannon. Somewhere there are tons of cannon balls, cannons, swivel guns, and the treasure they stored with it: the twenty tons of ivory said to have been on board, the casket of East Indian jewels, not to mention the rest of the coins . . . This didn't wash ashore; it sank in one big heap. Southack knew it. He said, "The riches with the guns will be buried in the sand."

One late afternoon I was visiting Chris, checking on progress. All around him, sixteen others were conserving and cataloging well over 100,000 objects. Three men at the other end of the room had raised a cannon from one of the tanks and were carefully removing a loose concretion from its muzzle. You never knew what you might find inside. As they pulled the concretion free, gas created by the electrolysis escaped, we all heard a loud pop, and before I even turned to look, the tompion—a wooden plug used to keep the gunpowder dry—shot across the room, caught me square on the knee, and dropped to the floor.

Chris was the first to gain his composure.

"There you have it," he said. "The last blast of the *Whydah* cannon."

•   •   •

But he was wrong.

In some ways the story of the *Whydah* ended, for me, on July 19, 1984. Nothing was quite the same after that. Though we celebrated then, now I think the earlier days, when we met on the lawn of the Captain's House before heading to the *Crumpstey*, all bound by a common goal, were the best.

There is nothing like a treasure hunt to bring out a person's true character. The crew often numbered too many would-be leaders and far too many eccentric independents. But most of the men exhibited a great spirit of courage and tenacity. Todd Murphy, a diving supervisor with a flawless record, and Stretch Gray, strong and capable, loyal in opposing any adversary—no captain could ask for more from his crewmen, or from his friends. Ken Kinkor, back on land, took our work and made Bellamy's world come alive. So, yes, business and scholarship can find a common ground. Still, today, I find myself neither the sad-eyed single parent Birgitta may have seen or the dreamer Heidi must have thought she'd found. I am a treasure hunter. I live my life on the edge between greed and friendship. Recognizing a friend from an enemy is more than half the job. Bellamy knew it, too: Treasure has the power to pull men apart, or join them in a common cause. It's not your average lifestyle.

Rob McClung and I finally had our falling out; we don't have much to say to each other. Birgitta is happily remarried, with a new daughter and a husband who enjoys gardening. I spend time with Brandon and Barry Jr., and not long ago I got a postcard from Jenny, a ski instructor in Colorado, asking me if I knew somebody had named a window after Trip Wheeler. Matt Costa, stubborn as ever, insists we never found the *Whydah*. My opinion? Well, you've heard the old saying, "Give a man enough rope . . ." I'll miss taking Costa on. Heidi moved to Los Angeles, where she met a struggling young writer. She's back on the cape now, modeling again. Her relationship with the writer fizzled after she came along with me on a preliminary treasure-hunting jaunt to Belize that lasted almost a month. We both know it would be better just to stay friends, but we're finding it hard to forget the romance of the *Whydah*.

I moved to a house with large windows that looks onto the ocean. "Beautiful place," a reporter said to me last week. "When are you moving in?" "I *am* moved in," I told him. "I live here." The truth is, it's where I pack my suitcase. Lately I've been shuttling back and forth between here and South America, a continent where surviving—never mind treasure hunting—is a daily adventure. There's no Board of Archaeological Resources to deal with down there; instead of calling lawyers, the locals reach for their knives and guns. It's a place where you know a man by the look in his eyes.

My advice? It's a mistake to think you can build some sort of stable life around treasure hunting. If you get the urge, you'd probably be best off selling your home, your car, any other unnecessary possessions, and dedicating yourself to the search—not the money, but the search. Most of the successful treasure hunters I know aren't wealthy men, and the vast majority of treasure hunters are unsuccessful. Better still, if you come down with whatever disease it is that makes people do things like this, spend your money on a psychologist. Because once you get started, there's no turning back.

Uncle Bill knew that. And he knew something else:

The real treasure is the story.

APPENDIX

❖

THE TREASURE

The following is a Manifest of Recovered Artifacts from the pirate ship Why-dah, *as of the time of publication. Many more artifacts will be catalogued as they come out of concretion, and as a result of future excavation of the shipwreck site.*

Artifact Type	Material	Count
ACTIVITIES		
### CARPENTRY TOOLS		
Adze	Composite	2
Awl	Composite	2
Ax	Composite	1
Ax handle	Wood	1
Caulking iron	Iron	2
Chisel	Wood	3
File	Latex	2
Hammer	Iron	4
Hammer handle	Wood	1
Hammer head	Latex	1
Maul	Iron	1
Plum	Lead	1
Prybar	Iron	1
Vice	Small concretion	1
### FISHING IMPLEMENTS		
Net weight	Lead	87
### HAND TOOLS		
Pin	Brass	77
Scissors	Brass	10
Seal	Silver	2

Artifact Type	Material	Count
Slate pencil	Slate	1
Stylus	Brass	2
Thread	Bast fiber	1
Other hand tools	Wood	5

MANUFACTURAL EQUIPMENT

Grinding stone	Other stone	1
Mortar	Brass	1

MANUFACTURAL WASTE

Other manufactural waste	Lead	292

MEASURING INSTRUMENTS

Weight	Brass	19

NAVIGATION INSTRUMENTS

Compass	Brass	10
Divider	Brass	4
Navigational rule	Composite	3
Ring dial	Brass	1
Sounding lead	Lead	3
Sounding lead rope	Bast fiber	1

RESTRAINING DEVICES

Leg iron	Medium Concretion	24

RIGGER/SAILMAKER TOOLS

Sail needle	Brass	1

TOOLS & IMPLEMENTS

Other/individual tools & implements	Latex	1

ARMS AND ARMAMENT

AMMUNITION

1-Pounder	Iron	13
2-Pounder	Iron	12
3-Pounder	Iron	25

Artifact Type	Material	Count
4-Pounder	Iron	76
6-Pounder	Iron	1
Bag shot (sewn together)	Composite	13
Bar shot	Iron	6
Bar shot 1-Pounder	Iron	2
Bar shot 2-Pounder	Medium concretion	2
Bar shot 3-Pounder	Iron	2
Bar shot 4-Pounder	Iron	8
Cannon wadding	Bast fiber	8
Expanding bar shot	Composite	5
Paper cartridge	Composite	4
Pistol wadding	Bast fiber	3
Round shot	Iron	8
Shot 1.00mm	Lead	1,529
Shot 1.18mm	Lead	2,879
Shot 1.40mm	Lead	2,084
Shot 1.70mm	Lead	502
Shot 11.2mm	Lead	90
Shot 12.5mm	Lead	307
Shot 13.2mm	Lead	1,253
Shot 16.0mm	Lead	1,344
Shot 19.0mm	Lead	45
Shot 2.00mm	Lead	1,654
Shot 2.36mm	Lead	1,832
Shot 2.80mm	Lead	11,476
Shot 3.35mm	Lead	12,273
Shot 4.00mm	Lead	43,301
Shot 5.60mm	Lead	177
Shot 6.30mm	Lead	8
Shot 6.70mm	Lead	2,669
Shot 8.00mm	Lead	4,317
Shot 9.50mm	Lead	53
Shot < 1.00mm	Lead	703
Other projectiles	Lead	41
Other shot	Lead	9

CANNON & COMPONENTS

Apron (touchhole cover)	Lead	13
Apron lash	Bast fiber	42

Artifact Type	*Material*	*Count*
3-Pound cannon	Iron	7
4-Pound cannon	Iron	15
6-Pound cannon	Iron	5
Cannon vent pick	Brass	2
Gun carriage (truck)	Wood	2
Tompion	Wood	7
Tompion cord	Bast fiber	1
Trunion cap	Iron	1
Trunion cap retaining key	Iron	2
Vent pick (priming wire)	Brass	9
Other cannon components	Iron	7

FIREARMS & COMPONENTS

Artifact Type	Material	Count
Butt plate	Brass	2
Carbine	Composite	1
Cloth handle wrap	Protein fiber	21
Cock vise jaw	Iron	7
Escutcheon plate	Brass	2
Foresight	Brass	4
Gun barrel	Composite	2
Gun barrel	Iron	24
Gun barrel	Medium concretion	26
Gun worm	Silver	5
Hand gun	Composite	2
Holster	Protein fiber	41
Lock cock	Iron	12
Lock flint	Chalcedony	4
Lock flint patch	Leather	27
Lock frizzen	Iron	3
Lock frizzen spring	Iron	2
Lock main spring	Iron	13
Lock plate	Latex	7
Lock plate (lock)	Latex	9
Lock plate (lock)	Latex	1
Lock plate screw	Iron	1
Lock screw	Iron	2
Lock sear	Iron	1
Lock sear	Latex	2

Artifact Type	*Material*	*Count*
Lock tumbler	Iron	6
Musket	Composite	5
Musket brace	Brass	1
Musket ramrod	Wood	4
Musket rest	Latex	3
Musket stock	Wood	11
Musket trigger plate	Brass	1
Pistol stock	Small concretion	2
Ramrod	Wood	3
Ramrod pipe	Brass	4
Ramrod pipe	Brass	11
Shotbag	Leather	1
Shotbag parts	Protein fiber	11
Side plate	Brass	4
Side plate	Brass	10
Sling retainer	Brass	2
Trigger guard	Brass	5
Trigger guard	Brass	14
Trigger plate	Brass	2
Vise jaw screw	Iron	1
Other arms accessories	Latex	9
Other arms components	Iron	9

SWORDS/BLADES

Blade	Iron	1
Blade	Iron	2
Blade	Medium concretion	2
Cutlass	Latex	1
Grip	Ivory	1
Grip	Wood	1
Hand guard	Latex	2
Hand guard	Silver	8
Hilt	Brass	2
Hilt	Latex	1
Pike pole	Wood	3
Pommel	Latex	1
Sword/blade belt hook	Silver	3

Artifact Type	Material	Count

WEAPONRY

Fuse	Wood	8
Grenade	Iron	16

CARGO

COIN

Bawbee	Copper	1
Coin cluster	Small concretion	8
½-Crown	Silver	1
Crown	Silver	1
½-Ecu	Silver	2
1-Ecu	Silver	1
1-Escudo	Gold	2
2-Escudo	Gold	5
8-Escudo	Gold	2
½-Real	Silver	751
1-Real	Silver	1,613
2-Real	Silver	2,257
4-Real	Silver	935
8-Real	Silver	2,795
Indeterminate reales	Silver	6
½-Shilling	Silver	1
15-Sou	Silver	2
20-Sou	Silver	3
30-Sou	Silver	2
Other coins	Copper	9

OTHER CURRENCY

Bit	Gold	6,174
Dust	Gold	1,518
Ingot/bar	Gold	17
Nugget	Gold	14
Indeterminate tokens	Lead	1

JEWELRY/ORNAMENTS

Bead	Gold	537
Filigree	Gold	4

Artifact Type	Material	Count
Pendant	Gold	2
Other ornaments	Gold	163

MERCHANDISE

Bale seal	Lead	12

STORAGE

Barrel	Level 1 concretion	2
Barrel stave	Wood	7
Other storage containers	Bast fiber	1

GALLEY

FAUNAL REMAINS

Other mammals	Bone	28

GALLEY/KITCHENWARE

Bottle	Glass	128
Bottle stopper	Cork	2
Coal fuel	Coal	31
Keg spigot	Brass	1
Kettle lug	Brass	2
Kettle rivet	Brass	21
Other preparation vessels	Medium concretion	1

TABLEWARE

Bowl	Earthenware	3
Fork	Iron	2
Knife handle	Wood	2
Plate	Pewter	8
Spoon	Pewter	7
Teapot	Pewter	1

PERSONAL OBJECTS

APPAREL

Buckle	Silver	73
Buck tang	Pewter	1

Artifact Type	*Material*	*Count*
Button	Silver	35
Clothes hook	Brass	4
Clothing	Bast fiber	153
Cuff link	Brass	14
Footwear	Leather	2
Sock	Protein fiber	1

JEWELRY/ORNAMENTS

Ring	Gold	1

PERSONAL OBJECTS

Bag	Composite	22

RECREATION

Gaming piece	Lead	28
Pipe bowl	Kaolin	5
Pipe stem 5/64	Kaolin	7
Pipe stem 6/64	Kaolin	2
Indeterminate pipe stems	Kaolin	3

SHIP ARCHITECTURE

FURNISHINGS & HARDWARE

Coat hook/peg	Iron	2
Knob/pull	Brass	3
Stud	Pewter	41

LIGHTING FIXTURES & HARDWARE

Candle holder	Pewter	1
Candle snuffer holder	Brass	1

OTHER HARDWARE

Hinge	Hysol	6
Washer	Iron	6
Wire	Brass	6
Other hardware	Latex	1

RIGGING ELEMENTS

Chain	Iron	1
Chain plate	Medium concretion	6

Artifact Type	Material	Count
Dead eye	Iron	8
Hawser-laid	Bast fiber	1
Rams head block	Medium concretion	1
Rope	Bast fiber	22
Single sheave block	Medium concretion	2
Indeterminate cordage	Bast fiber	57

SHIP STRUCTURE/COMPONENTS

Artifact Type	Material	Count
Bilge pump (piston)	Wood	1
Bolt	Latex	3
Bower anchor	Iron	1
Bower anchor ring	Iron	1
Chock	Iron	1
Drift pin	Hysol	3
Eye bolt	Iron	2
Fire brick	Brick	3
Handwrought nail	Iron	76
Hoist hook	Latex	1
Indeterminate nails	Hysol	42
Kedge anchor	Iron	1
Kedge anchor ring	Iron	1
Keel spike	Medium concretion	4
Patch	Lead	15
Pintle hinge	Iron	1
Pissoir	Lead	1
Planking	Wood	2
Roll	Lead	6
Scupper liner	Lead	4
Ship bell	Composite	1
Spike	Iron	92
Strap	Latex	18
Tack	Iron	30
Other hull fasteners	Hysol	2
Other nautical bells	Bronze	1
Other ship components	Wood	1
Other ship structures/ components	Wood	9

STRUCTURAL MATERIAL

Artifact Type	Material	Count
Sheet	Copper	1

Artifact Type	*Material*	*Count*
OTHER		
	DOCUMENTATION	
Documentation	Latex	2
	FAUNAL REMAINS	
Bird	Bone	3
Fish	Bone	15
Human	Bone	1
Indeterminate shells	Shell	14
Other/indeterminate faunal remains	Shell	2
	FLORAL REMAINS	
Seeds/nuts	Other organic	1
Other/indeterminate floral remains	Other organic	1
	MODERN INTRUSIVE	
Fishing line swivel	Brass	1
Modern intrusive artifact	Aluminum	73
Modern projectile	Brass	302
Other/individual modern intrusive	Other metal	4
	SAMPLE	
Sample	Gunpowder	22
	INDETERMINATE	
Indeterminate curved	Lead	10
Indeterminate flat	Iron	20
Indeterminate fragments	Lead	52
Indeterminate rounded	Iron	38
Other indeterminate	Wood	1,257

INDEX